DOING BUSINESS INTERNATIONALLY

THE CROSS-CULTURAL CHALLENGES©

PARTICIPANT WORKBOOK

P T P

PRINCETON TRAINING PRESS

A DIVISION OF TRAINING MANAGEMENT CORPORATION

DOING BUSINESS INTERNATIONALLY

THE CROSS-CULTURAL CHALLENGES©

Executive Director: Danielle Walker
Writer/Program Designer: Terence Brake
Assistant Writer: Kim Sullivan

Video Production: MultiMedia, Inc.

245 Nassau Street, Princeton, NJ 08542 U.S.A.
Phone (609) 497-1290
Fax (609) 497-1295

Call us with questions, suggestions, or orders!

FIRST PRINTING: SEPTEMBER 1992

ISBN: 1-882390-00-8

Acknowledgements

We wish to express our appreciation to the following training professionals for their generous support and encouragement of this project:

Serge Ogranovitch (Potomack Partnership)
Stephen H. Rhinesmith (Rhinesmith and Associates, Inc.)
Diane Simpson (Simpson International, Inc.)

P T P

PRINCETON TRAINING PRESS
A DIVISION OF TRAINING MANAGEMENT CORPORATION

TABLE OF CONTENTS

TMC and PTP Overview		I
Using this Workbook		II
Rationale: The Global Business Challenge		III
Objectives		IV
Module Overviews		V
Program Map		VII
Module 1:	**Global Business Thinking**	1-1
Unit A:	Going Global: Changes in the Marketplace	1-2
Unit B:	Doing Business in New Ways	1-17
Module 2:	**Cross-Cultural Awareness**	2-1
Unit A:	What Is Culture?	2-2
Unit B:	Developing Cross-Cultural Effectiveness	2-27
Module 3:	**Cross-Cultural Communication**	3-1
Unit A:	The Communication Process	3-2
Unit B:	Doing Things Differently: Business & Social Etiquette	3-14
Unit C:	Handling Cross-Cultural Differences	3-18
Module 4:	**Working Across Cultures**	4-1
Unit A:	Culture and Management	4-2
Unit B:	Adapting Business Skills	4-21
Unit C:	Marketing and Sales	4-27
Unit D:	The International Manager: Success Factors	4-39
Appendix A:	Useful Resources	A1
Appendix B:	Regional Cultural Profiles	B1
Appendix C:	Selected Country Information	C1
Appendix D:	Exercises: Suggested Answers	D1

TMC AND PTP OVERVIEW

Training Management Corporation (TMC) is an international full-service training consulting firm that specializes in course design and program management. TMC takes a consultative approach to training assignments with the understanding that training interventions have broad-based organizational implications that may require additional efforts in areas such as team building, process institutionalization and other organizational development initiatives. TMC focuses in four areas: Management, Supervisory, Global Management and Project/Quality Management.

Founded in 1984, TMC now offers its consulting and training programs worldwide. To date, thousands of participants from companies in fields as diverse as electronics, defense, information technology and services, petrochemicals, finance, pharmaceuticals, consumer products, engineering, and telecommunications have benefited from TMC's services and programs. TMC has also developed training curricula for various government agencies and academic institutions.

A partial listing of TMC clients includes: American Express, ARCO International Oil and Gas, AT&T, Bristol-Myers Squibb, Chase Manhattan Bank, Chemical Bank, Citicorp, Colgate-Palmolive, DuPont, the Ford Foundation, Foster Wheeler, Glaxo, HIMONT, Hoechst-Celanese, Hoffmann-La Roche, Johnson & Johnson, Merck, Mobil, the New York City Transit Authority, NYNEX, Paine Webber, Philips Electronics, Pioneer Hi-Bred International, Princeton University, Prudential, Prudential Securities, Rhone Poulenc-Rorer, and Westinghouse.

Princeton Training Press (PTP) is the publishing division of Training Management Corporation. Its mission is to publish high quality professional development products – for large and small businesses – that are practical, comprehensive, easy to use, and affordable. Its publishing focus is on the creation of training tools in major areas of international and domestic business, including: global management, multi-cultural teamwork, project management, managerial and supervisory skills, business communications, and sales and marketing.

USING THIS WORKBOOK

The **Doing Business Internationally** training package contains two items: an introductory video and a workbook. While the video and the workbook have been designed to complement one another, they are independent, self-standing learning tools. The video provides an overview of key topic areas and the workbook offers a detailed instructional guide to the impact of culture on business activities.

The Participant Workbook can be used in a number of ways:

- **Self-Study:** The workbook is designed so that you can study the contents by yourself at your own pace. The contents are organized in a logical flow, and key points are reinforced with real-life examples and practical exercises. This method is most beneficial for those who are unable – through work pressure or remote location – to attend a company training session.

- **Partnering:** As an extension of the above, working with another individual, or small group of individuals, can add support and challenge as you explore the complex world of cultural differences. Choosing partners with different cultural orientations is most beneficial.

- **Group Sessions:** Led by an experienced facilitator, you and your colleagues can work together on individual, group, and company issues related to doing business in the international marketplace. This method allows for the greatest sharing of perspectives, and provides the greatest opportunity for individual and organizational learning. To gain maximum benefits, be open to examining your own cultural background as well as to sharing any experiences you have in managing day-to-day international business.

Note: The workbook contains two types of questions - Review Questions and Study Questions.

- **Review Questions:** No answers to these questions are given in the workbook. These questions have been included in the text for you and colleagues to analyze and discuss. They relate to applying key concepts to yourself or your company.

- **Study Questions:** These aim to reinforce your understanding of the material. Suggested answers to these questions are given in Appendix D.

RATIONALE: THE GLOBAL BUSINESS CHALLENGE

What is the Global Business Challenge?

Are you ready to meet the cross-cultural challenges of international business?

Having the ability to manage and do business with people from different parts of the world is no longer a *nice skill to have*; it is a *necessity*. The urgency in the business community to find and develop individuals who can be successful at the international level is not just another fad. It is a question of economic survival.

How can companies be competitive in today's marketplace? They *must* be able to:

- Provide the highest quality products and services
- To the most profitable world-wide markets
- At the lowest cost
- Under dynamic and challenging market and competitive conditions
- Through the global sourcing of raw materials, technology, capital, facilities, and human resources.

The world has experienced tremendous change in recent years. The Cold War has ended; old empires have crumbled and new economies have emerged in their own right. Some trade barriers have fallen while new powerful trading blocs are forging alliances. The intensity and the speed of changes in world markets mean that organizations, and their managers, must have the flexibility, confidence, and skills needed to overcome increased competitive pressures, pursue expanded opportunities, and grow market share. Instantaneous communications have rapidly increased the flow of business transactions across continents, and new technologies continue to transform product development and manufacturing processes. In addition, corporate mergers and joint ventures in the international arena are challenging individuals to find ways to work productively across many nations and cultures.

A key to success in the global market is the development of international managers who can cross geographic, functional, and cultural boundaries and maximize synergies.

In sum, traditional markets and businesses are being transformed and the race is on to succeed in this new world economy.

OBJECTIVES

What does the Global Business Challenge mean to you?

To conduct business successfully in the international environment, you must be able to recognize and act on global opportunities and work effectively with people from different cultural backgrounds.

This program is a *foundation* course for building the skills you need to operate successfully in a variety of cultural settings and meet the global business challenge. You will sharpen those perceptual, listening, and observational skills critical to functioning effectively in unfamiliar business environments as well as learn about significant global trends and major cultural regions.

After completing this program, you will be able to:

- Analyze key global trends and their impact on current business practices.
- Recognize the impact of cultural differences on business relationships.
- Identify and overcome intercultural communication barriers in order to achieve greater effectiveness and synergy.
- Adapt key business skills to maximize effectiveness when working across different cultures.

These are difficult tasks. Developing the expertise to transfer business skills across regional and business cultures is an *ongoing* challenge. Think of the **Doing Business Internationally** program as a first step. The most important success factor in doing business in other countries will be your *commitment to continuous learning*.

Good luck. We are confident you will profit by taking this first step.

MODULE OVERVIEWS

MODULE 1: GLOBAL BUSINESS THINKING

For organizations and their managers to survive and flourish in the 1990's and on into the twenty-first century, a global perspective must be adopted. Accelerating developments in technology, world markets, and competitive positions are driving radical changes in how we need to think and act in the business environment. The evolution of companies from domestic to global involves major changes in business organizations and activities. To succeed in this complex global system, managers must understand, and stay in touch with, significant global trends; examine their own businesses in relation to the dynamics of globalization; and rethink their roles and values to meet the challenges of greater diversity, complexity, and uncertainty.

MODULE 2: CROSS-CULTURAL AWARENESS

As a company moves onto the international playing field, culture comes to play an extremely important role in business success.

Culture is the code of behaviors, values, beliefs, and patterns of thinking that we learn as we grow and develop in our social groups. Culture determines how we view ourselves and others, how we behave, and how we perceive the world around us. We tend to believe that our way of seeing is the only way, or at least the best.

Although cultures can vary in dramatic ways, we can profile cultures according to their relationship to ten key variables: Nature, Time, Action, Communication, Space, Power, Individualism, Competitiveness, Structure, and Formality. These variables provide us with a frame of reference for understanding the characteristics of different cultures and adapting behaviors. The role of culture in doing business effectively becomes increasingly important as a company evolves into a global entity. Developing cultural effectiveness in business involves a three step process: Self-Awareness, Cross-Cultural Understanding, and Adapting Business Skills.

MODULE OVERVIEWS (Cont'd)

MODULE 3: CROSS-CULTURAL COMMUNICATION

Communication takes place when you share the same meaning with someone else. This can be difficult with someone from your own culture. The difficulties are often multiplied many times over when you're trying to communicate with someone from another culture. You cannot assume that what is "common sense" to you is "common sense" to someone else. Appropriate colors to wear can be important if you are not to offend your host; the same gesture of the hand can mean O.K. in one culture and be obscene in another; inquiring about female members of a family may be considered very impolite in some cultures and friendly in others. While understanding the cross-cultural communication process is very helpful, you also need to be prepared to handle cross-cultural differences and adapt your negotiation style to fit the situation. We will all make mistakes when doing business internationally; the critical factors are to minimize the number of mistakes we make, learn from those we do make, and move on more effectively.

MODULE 4: WORKING ACROSS CULTURES

You may be sent to work overseas on a lengthy assignment. You may lead a project team that has members from a number of foreign subsidiaries. You may make a relatively short trip to another country to troubleshoot a problem. In all such cases, you need to prepare yourself to cope with diversity. You are accustomed to performing your management functions within your own culture. You and your employees share similar expectations and values. Within a foreign culture, how will you plan, organize, staff, lead, and control? What adjustments will you need to make? How will you market and sell across different cultural terrain? Learning how to learn is critical for the international manager: continuous learning from people, places, books, newspapers and other resources is a must.

PROGRAM MAP

WORK THROUGH EACH MODULE AND UNIT IN SEQUENCE.

MODULE 1: GLOBAL BUSINESS THINKING

Primary Objective: Analyze key global trends and their impact on current business practices.

Units:
A. Going Global: Changes In The Marketplace
B. Doing Business In New Ways

MODULE 2: CROSS-CULTURAL AWARENESS

Primary Objective: Recognize the impact of cultural differences on business relationships.

Units:
A. What Is Culture?
B. Developing Cultural Effectiveness

MODULE 3: CROSS-CULTURAL COMMUNICATION

Primary Objective: Identify and overcome intercultural communication barriers in order to achieve greater effectiveness and synergy.

Units:
A. The Communication Process
B. Doing Things Differently: Business And Social Etiquette
C. Handling Cross-Cultural Differences

MODULE 4: WORKING ACROSS CULTURES

Primary Objective: Adapt key business skills to maximize effectiveness when working across different cultures.

Units:
A. Culture And Management
B. Adapting Business Skills
C. Marketing And Sales
D. The International Manager: Success Factors

NOTES

MODULE 1: GLOBAL BUSINESS THINKING

Overview

Primary Objective: Analyze key global trends and their impact on current business practices.

Units:

A: Going Global: Changes In the Marketplace

B: Doing Business In New Ways

For organizations and their managers to survive and flourish in the 1990's and on into the twenty-first century, a global perspective must be adopted. Accelerating developments in technology, world markets, and competitive positions are driving radical changes in how we need to think and act in the business environment. The evolution of companies from domestic to global involves major changes in business organizations and activities. To succeed in this complex global system, managers must understand, and stay in touch with, significant global trends; examine their own businesses in relation to the dynamics of globalization; and rethink their roles and values to meet the challenges of greater diversity, complexity, and uncertainty.

UNIT A: GOING GLOBAL: CHANGES IN THE MARKETPLACE

Objectives

After completing this unit, you will be able to:

 Identify the agenda for global competitiveness

 Identify the major forces driving the move to globalization

 Identify the critical business needs making a global perspective urgent

 Recognize the key levels in the evolution of international business and the characteristics of each level

THE COMPETITIVE AGENDA

To be competitive in today's business environment, companies must provide:

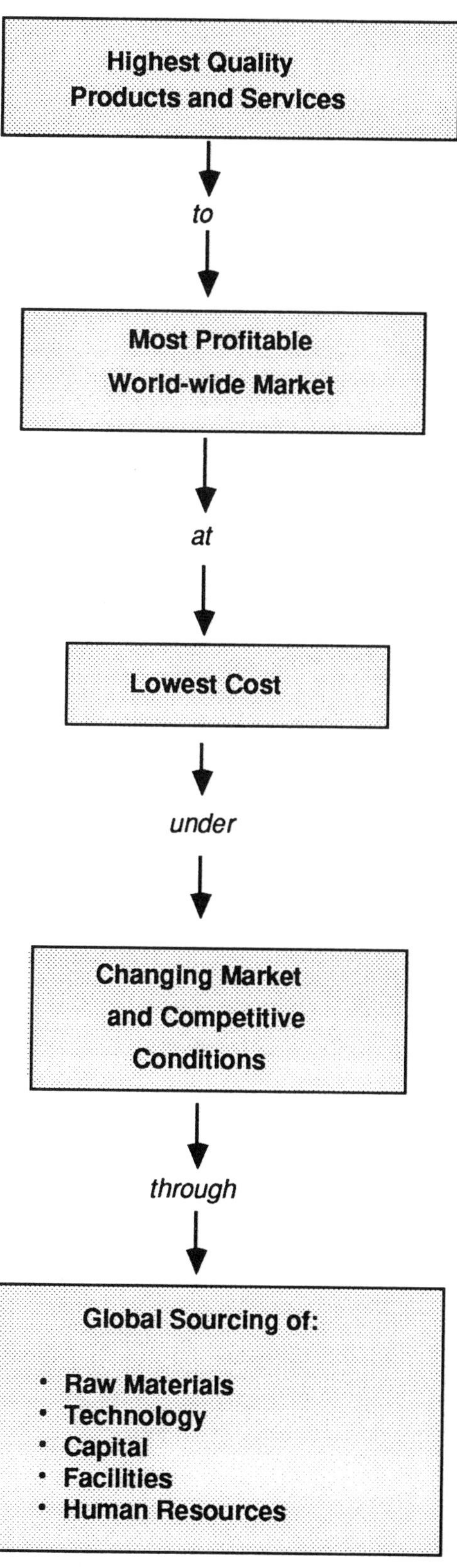
Highest Quality
Products and Services
to
Most Profitable
World-wide Market
at
Lowest Cost
under
Changing Market
and Competitive
Conditions
through
Global Sourcing of:
• Raw Materials
• Technology
• Capital
• Facilities
• Human Resources

GLOBAL SOURCING IN ACTION

In search of efficiencies and quality, auto companies are using components and expertise from across the globe. One European manufacturer – for its most popular compact car – brings together items from the following fifteen countries:

Country	Items
Austria	Tires, radiator and heater hoses.
Belgium	Tires, tubes, seat pads, brakes, trim.
Canada	Glass, radio.
Denmark	Fan belt.
France	Alternator, cylinder head, master cylinder, brakes, underbody coating, weatherstrips, clutch release bearings, steering shaft and joints, seat pads and frames, transmission cases, clutch cases, tires, suspension bushes, ventilation units, heater, hose clamps, sealers, hardware.
Germany	Locks, pistons, exhaust, ignition, switches, front disc, distributor, weatherstrips, rocker arm, speedometer, fuel tank, cylinder bolt, cylinder head gasket, front wheel knuckles, rear wheel spindle, transmission cases, clutch cases, clutch steering column, battery, glass.
Italy	Cylinder head, carburetor, glass, defroster grills.
Japan	Starter, alternator, cone and roller bearings, windshield, washer pump.
Netherlands	Tires, paints, hardware.
Norway	Exhaust flanges, tires.
Spain	Wiring harness, radiator and heater, hoses, fork clutch release, air filter, battery, mirrors.
Sweden	Hose clamps, cylinder bolt, exhaust down pipes, pressings, hardware.
Switzerland	Underbody coating, speedometer gears.
United Kingdom	Carburetor, rocker arm, clutch, ignition, exhaust, oil pump, distributor, cylinder bolt, cylinder head, flywheel ring gear, heater, speedometer, battery, rear wheel spindle, intake manifold, fuel tank, switches, lamps, front disc, steering wheel, steering column, glass, weatherstrips, locks.
United States	BGR valves, wheel nuts, hydraulic tappet glass.

Adapted from: Peter Dicken, *Global Shift: Industrial Change in a Turbulent World,* London: Harper and Row, 1986.

FORCES AT WORK

International business is now **the** topic for discussion in corporate boardrooms around the globe. There is a realization that the business environment is changing beyond recognition and will never be the same again. New technology is shortening product life cycles, markets are shifting, competitors are going everywhere, and quality is increasingly an issue. Companies can no longer rely on established market niches. Some of the major forces driving this change are:

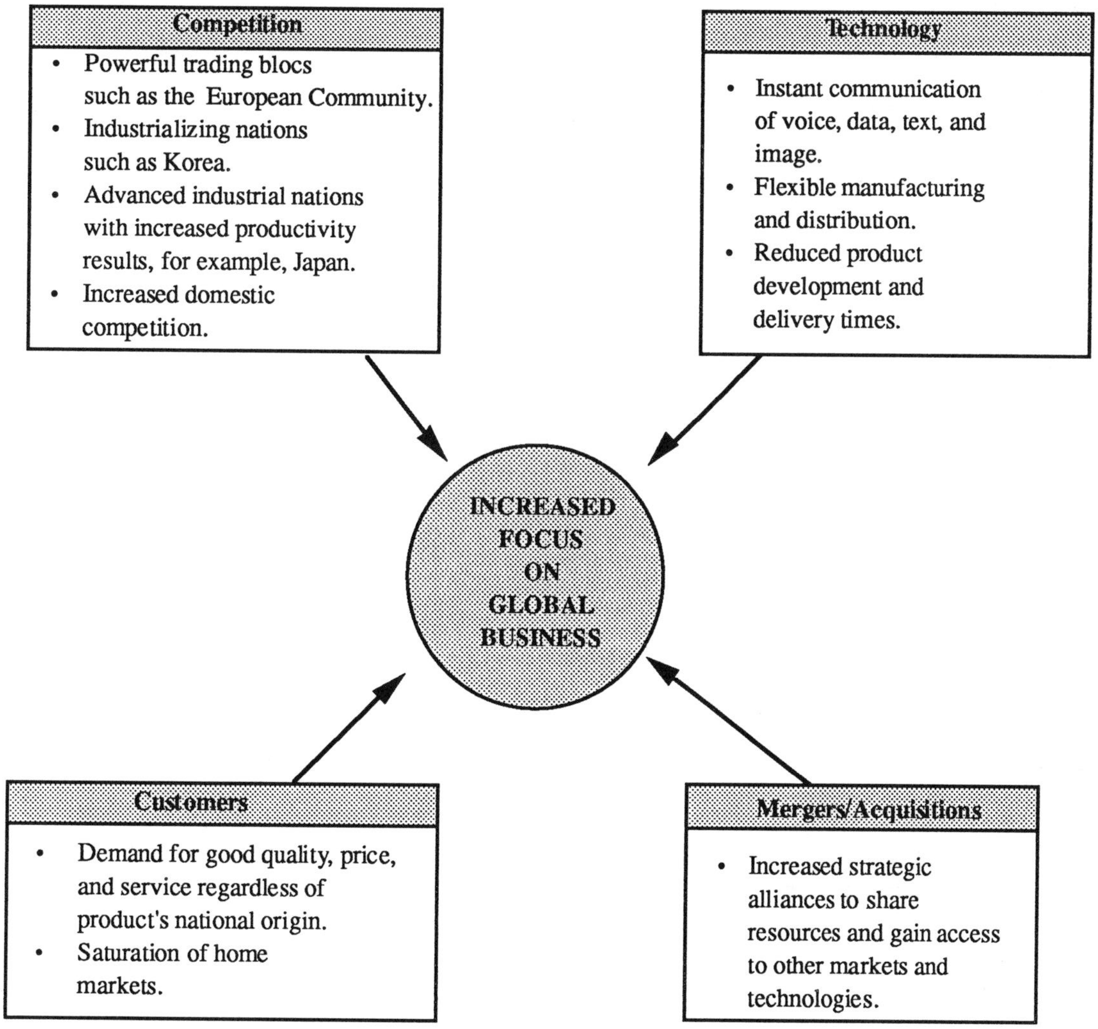

Competition

- Powerful trading blocs such as the European Community.
- Industrializing nations such as Korea.
- Advanced industrial nations with increased productivity results, for example, Japan.
- Increased domestic competition.

Technology

- Instant communication of voice, data, text, and image.
- Flexible manufacturing and distribution.
- Reduced product development and delivery times.

INCREASED FOCUS ON GLOBAL BUSINESS

Customers

- Demand for good quality, price, and service regardless of product's national origin.
- Saturation of home markets.

Mergers/Acquisitions

- Increased strategic alliances to share resources and gain access to other markets and technologies.

Review Question 1:

Think about your own industry/company. Which forces do you think are causing the most significant changes in your own business environment?

KEY GLOBAL PLAYERS: RELATIVE COMPETITIVENESS

Which nations are winning the competitive race in the global market? The bigger the box, the more competitive the country.

New Industrial States

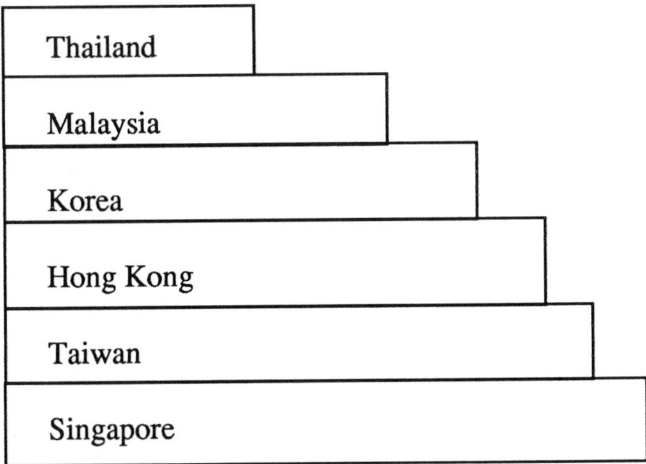

Established Industrial States

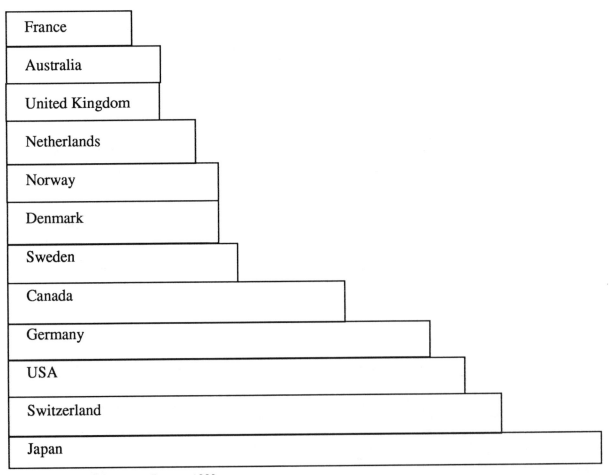

France
Australia
United Kingdom
Netherlands
Norway
Denmark
Sweden
Canada
Germany
USA
Switzerland
Japan

Source: *World Competitiveness Report*, 1990.

RACE AGAINST TIME

A key factor in global competitiveness is the product cycle – the amount of time it takes to develop a new product and get it to market.

Japan has taken the lead in the speed of new product development.

Activity	West	Japan
• Sales, order and distribution cycle for an automobile.	16-26 days	6-8 days
• Vehicle manufacture.	14-30 days	2-4 days
• New vehicle design and introduction.	4-6 years	2 1/2-3 years

Source: G. Stalk and T.M. Hout, *Competing Against Time: How Time-Based Competition is Reshaping Global Market,* The Free Press, New York, 1990.

DRIVING NEEDS FOR A GLOBAL BUSINESS PERSPECTIVE

The need for companies to globalize is driven by the following three primary needs:

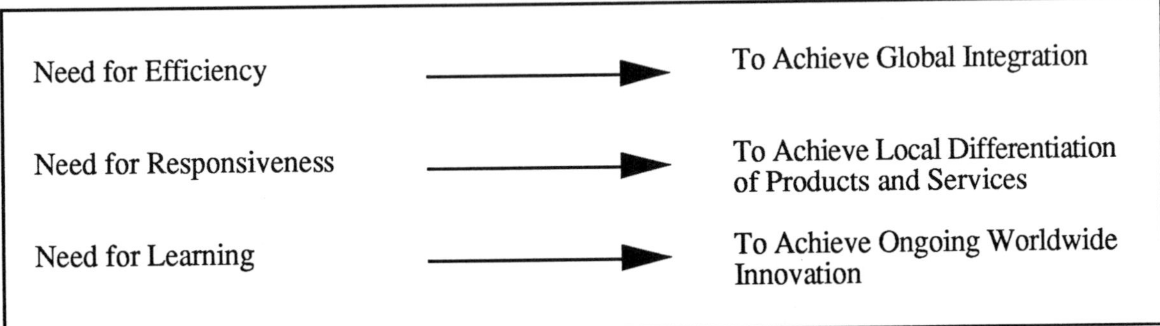

Only a corporation with a global strategy, structure, corporate culture and cadre of managers with an international perspective can effectively balance and achieve these needs.

To be simultaneously "global" (i.e., centralized or integrated for efficiency on a global or headquarters basis) and "local" (i.e., decentralized or differentiated for customer responsiveness on a country or subsidiary basis) is a major challenge for companies engaged in globalization. Furthermore, the need for worldwide innovation can only be achieved by managing the balance and flow of "global" and "local" information, technology, and learning.

CRITICAL BUSINESS AREAS

The needs for Efficiency, Responsiveness, and Learning are driving many companies to rethink three critical areas of their business:

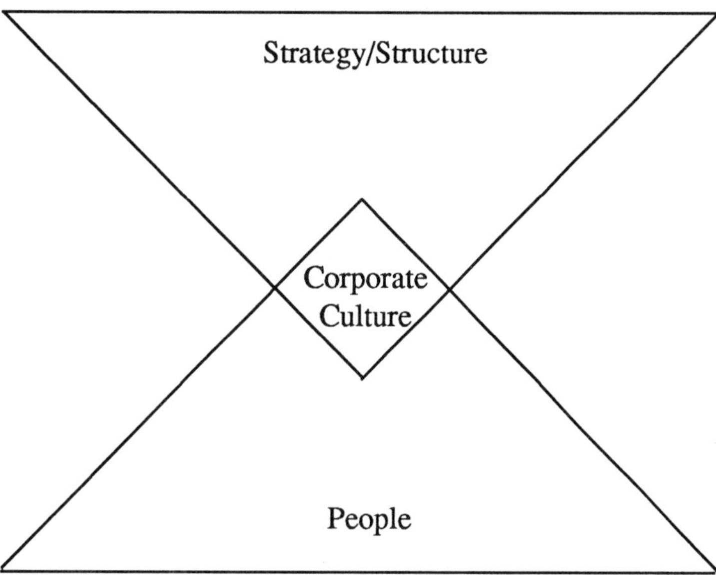

Adapted from: Stephen H. Rhinesmith, *"An Agenda For Globalization,"* Training and Development Journal, February 1991.

- **Strategy/Structure:** Develop global strategies/structures that create the organizational conditions and linkages needed to surface and balance conflicting demands. At headquarters and in affiliates, everyone must be clear about decision-making authority, i.e., who should be consulted? informed? who decides? which businesses, functions and tasks should be centralized and which should be decentralized?

- **Corporate Culture:** Develop a corporate culture that provides managers with the leadership support and management processes needed to complement global strategies and operate within a global organizational structure effectively.

- **People:** Provide training and development opportunities for managers and create a cadre of leaders with the mindsets and skills needed to manage on a global basis.

Companies tend to be good at determining appropriate strategies and structure. They are often less good at creating a cohesive corporate culture, and mobilizing people.

EVOLUTION OF INTERNATIONAL BUSINESS

A business goes through the following four distinct and progressively complex stages as it evolves from a successful domestic organization to a global corporation:

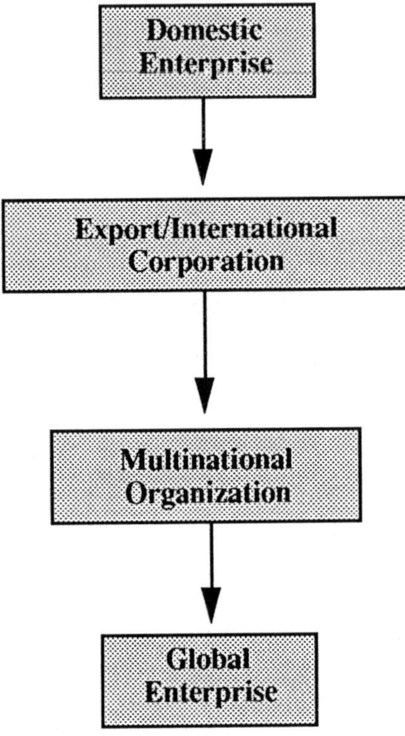

(Pages 1-11 to 1-15 are adapted from "*Developing Leaders for the Global Enterprise,*" by Stephen H. Rhinesmith, Training and Development Journal, April 1989.)

DOMESTIC

A domestic company is defined primarily according to where it sells its products. Even domestic companies, however, need to scan the global environment for trends and opportunities and source internationally.

Domestic Company Characteristics

The domestic company:

- Operates only within its own country.
- Uses domestic suppliers and produces and markets its services and products to customers at home.
- Collects and uses information only on domestic market trends, resources and environmental conditions.
- Has competitive strategies, plans and tactics that operate inside a domestic marketplace orientation.
- Organizes and re-organizes resources, technologies, marketing/distribution systems, networks, operating systems, etc., in response to local competitive and market changes.
- Creates, organizes and manages cross-functional teams as its central operating mode.
- Protects itself against unpredictable change by being highly flexible.
- Requires its managers to understand themselves and their associates.

Increasingly, domestically-focused companies are finding themselves losing market share to foreign competitors. Traditional markets are being broken up and the distinction between "domestic" and "international" is becoming increasingly irrelevant.

EXPORT/INTERNATIONAL

Export organizations have a product, service or technology that they export through distributors, but they have no - or very few - personnel overseas. International organizations have an international division, the members of which travel and work overseas. In addition, international companies may manufacture abroad.

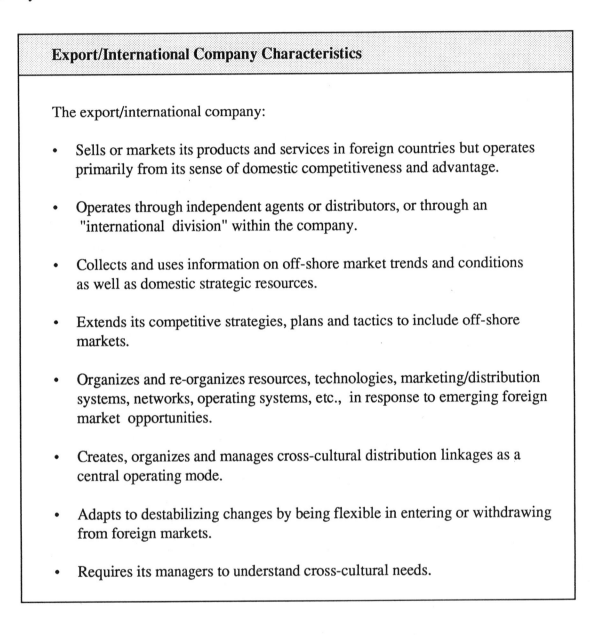

Export/International Company Characteristics

The export/international company:

- Sells or markets its products and services in foreign countries but operates primarily from its sense of domestic competitiveness and advantage.
- Operates through independent agents or distributors, or through an "international division" within the company.
- Collects and uses information on off-shore market trends and conditions as well as domestic strategic resources.
- Extends its competitive strategies, plans and tactics to include off-shore markets.
- Organizes and re-organizes resources, technologies, marketing/distribution systems, networks, operating systems, etc., in response to emerging foreign market opportunities.
- Creates, organizes and manages cross-cultural distribution linkages as a central operating mode.
- Adapts to destabilizing changes by being flexible in entering or withdrawing from foreign markets.
- Requires its managers to understand cross-cultural needs.

MULTINATIONAL

The multinational organizational form was pioneered in Europe by Philips and ICI. Until the 1980's, the multinational corporation was seen as the final stage of organizational development.

Multinational Company Characteristics

The multinational corporation:

- Is characterized by a centralized parent company that controls strategy, technology and resource allocation, as well as by localized national or regional operations that handle decisions regarding marketing, sales, manufacturing, customer service, and competitive tactics.
- Has national or regional operations that act independently of one another, usually communicating only back to headquarters/parent company.
- Collects and uses information on multi-domestic trends, environmental conditions, and strategic resources.
- Adapts their successful domestic market model to cultural contexts.
- Adapts systems and processes to international competitive conditions.
- Develops multinational alliances and ventures; manages cross-cultural work teams.
- Responds and adapts to destabilizing change by being flexible in reallocating resources across national markets.
- Requires its managers to work effectively in cross-cultural situations.

GLOBAL

Global companies seek to balance structure and flexibility, global and local needs, and on-time product delivery with low costs. This mix of integration and differentiation suggests a key competency for the international manager – managing complexity.

Global Company Characteristics

The global corporation:

- Is an extension of the multinational organization, but national or regional boundaries are no longer barriers, i.e., decisions are made to deliver products in the best markets, at the lowest cost, with the most appropriate management resources regardless of where funds, people, resources, technology, etc., reside.
- Represents a shift from the hierarchical multinational model to a flexible, entrepreneurial, networked model.
- Combines a centralized global strategic intent and/or a broad-based resource, technology and marketing allocation scheme with a localized customer focus and competitiveness that is responsive to regional or local conditions.
- Collects and uses information on global trends, conditions, and resources.
- Integrates holistic competitive strategies.
- Creates free-flowing resource allocation schemes.
- Creates global strategic partnerships – inter- and intra-organizational linkages.
- Creates destablized conditions in order to be proactive in the marketplace and gain advantages.
- Requires that its managers be able to manage and transcend cultural differences effectively .

It is very important for these companies to establish a global mission, values and vision, i.e., create a global corporate culture. With a strong global corporate culture, it is more likely that individuals across the world will consistently make the right decisions because they understand values of the organization.

MULTINATIONAL VS. GLOBAL ORGANIZATIONS

The critical differences between a multinational and a global company can be summarized as follows:

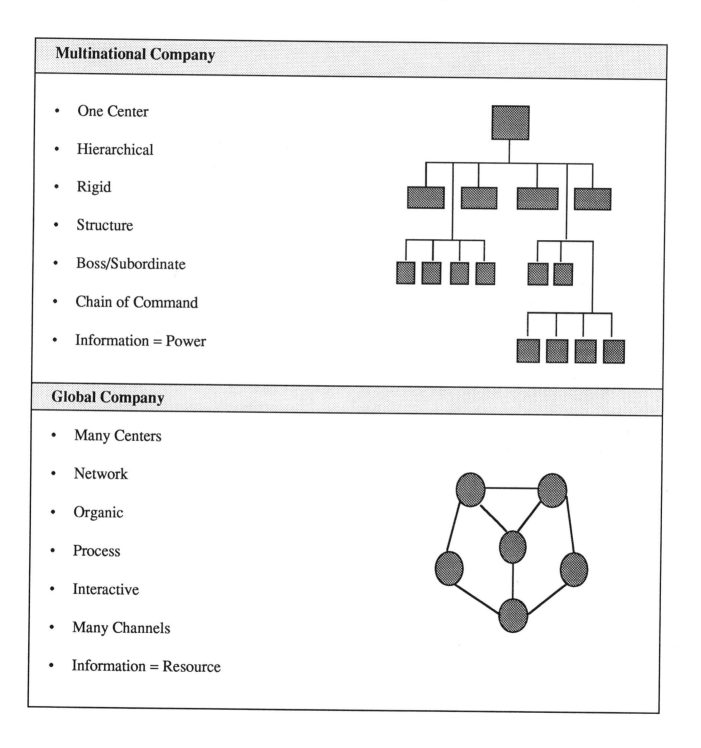

Multinational Company

- One Center
- Hierarchical
- Rigid
- Structure
- Boss/Subordinate
- Chain of Command
- Information = Power

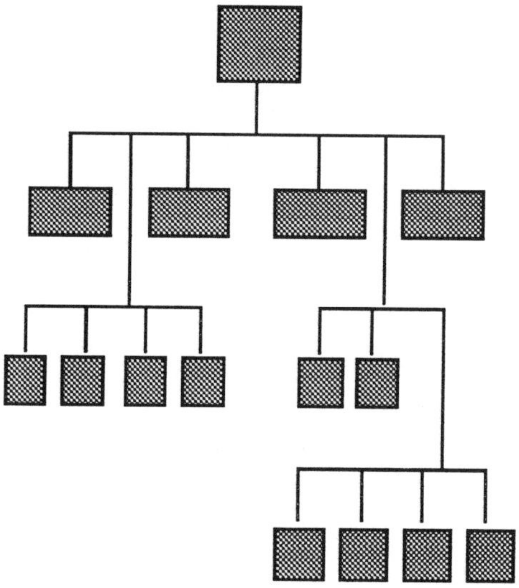

Global Company

- Many Centers
- Network
- Organic
- Process
- Interactive
- Many Channels
- Information = Resource

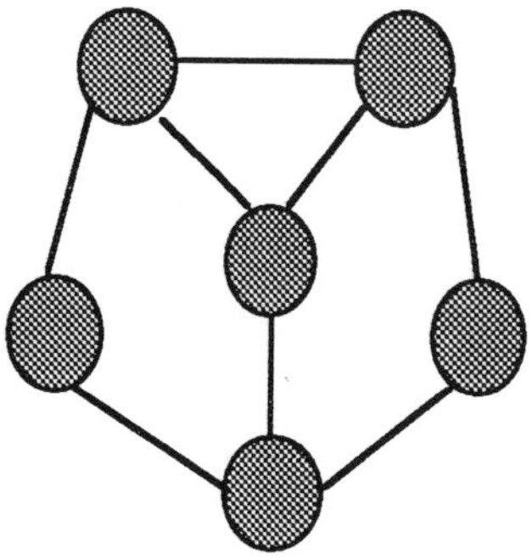

WHERE DO YOU FIT IN?

Take a few minutes to review this unit and then consider the following questions:

Review Question 2:

Where would you place your company in the globalization process?
(Domestic, Export/International, Multinational, Global)

Review Question 3:

What factors determined your choice?

Review Question 4:

Where would you like your company to be in the globalization process in five years? Why?

Review Question 5:

What changes to your organization's strategy/structure, corporate culture, and people might be necessary to move it to where you want it to be?

UNIT B: DOING BUSINESS IN NEW WAYS

Objectives

After completing this unit, you will be able to:

 Recognize the need to shift from a domestic to a global paradigm.

 Determine the key skills for identifying global trends and opportunities.

 Identify your priorities for developing global business thinking.

MAKING A PARADIGM SHIFT

What is a paradigm?

- A paradigm is how we "see" the world in terms of perceiving, understanding, interpreting – our mental map. Related terms are: model, theory, perception, assumption, frame of reference.

A global paradigm can be compared to a more domestic paradigm. The domestic paradigm is perfectly legitimate for a domestic organization but inappropriate for an organization that wants to compete in the global business environment. The contrast might look like the following:

Domestic Manager Paradigm	Global Manager Paradigm
• Works with narrow perspective, parochial interests.	• Drives for the bigger picture and global opportunities.
• Seeks to achieve functional, specialized expertise.	• Seeks to achieve cross-functional and cross-cultural expertise.
• Uses linear, analytic thinking.	• Uses non-linear, holistic thinking (systems).
• Has single-focus task accomplishment.	• Has multi-focus task accomplishment.
• Trusts structure, roles, responsibilities over process.	• Trusts process rather than structure.
• Values individual mastery and competence.	• Values teamwork, diversity, and experimentation.
• Avoids surprises; change is threatening.	• Sees change as opportunity.
• Seeks to eliminate conflict; views conflict as abnormal.	• Sees conflict as opportunity for synergy and enhanced decision making; views conflict as normal.
• Has win-lose, either/or mindset.	• Has win-win, balancing of conflicting positions mindset.

Review Question 6:

Imagine that you are an internal business consultant. You have been asked by senior management to describe your company (or division) in terms of the two paradigms. What would you report?

GLOBAL BUSINESS THINKING: THE CHANGE CHALLENGE

Change is increasingly rapid, disruptive, and complex. It can energize or paralyze individuals and organizations. Change is both creative and destructive; it can be messy and frightening. Yet, it is an opportunity for innovation and breakthrough accomplishments, and these are key to lasting success in the marketplace.

The shift from a domestic to a global paradigm involves both organizational and individual change. Neither is a simple A to Z process.

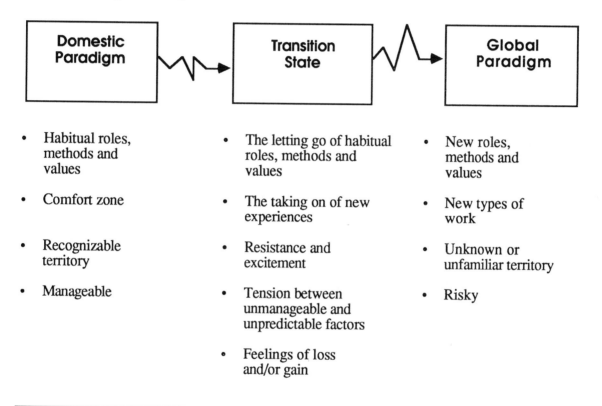

- Habitual roles, methods and values
- Comfort zone
- Recognizable territory
- Manageable

- The letting go of habitual roles, methods and values
- The taking on of new experiences
- Resistance and excitement
- Tension between unmanageable and unpredictable factors
- Feelings of loss and/or gain

- New roles, methods and values
- New types of work
- Unknown or unfamiliar territory
- Risky

Review Question 7:

What do you think are the major challenges you and your company face in shifting to a global paradigm?

KEEPING IN TOUCH: THE ENVIRONMENTAL SCAN

A key part of managing the change is staying in touch with key issues and trends. This involves performing a number of practices and tasks on a regular basis.

Definition

An environmental scan combines the gathering of information on an international basis and the capacity to use the information to increase the profitability of the organization. The information may be financial, political, cultural, technological, or marketing-related.

Key Practices and Tasks

Practice #1: Set *critical success factors* (CSFs) for the organization's international competitiveness and use these as a framework to filter information for key trends.

- Determine the most important tasks to be done in your job to ensure that your function is managed well on a cross-functional and international basis.
- Use CSFs as a framework to search on a global basis for and filter information that will affect your ability to be successful in your job responsibilities.

Practice #2: Establish *personal and organizational information systems* that scan for trends, best practices and resources which provide new opportunities for increased competitive advantage.

- Read professional and commercial publications that track your functional and industry trends and practices on an international, rather than national, basis.
- Join professional associations and attend meetings and conferences that stress the international aspects of your job responsibilities.
- Search for best practices in your job on a global basis, both within your organization and within your industry or profession.
- Develop at least one new idea each year to increase your productivity or your organization's competitiveness, the seeds of which were obtained from outside your country.

KEEPING IN TOUCH: THE ENVIRONMENTAL SCAN (Cont'd)

Practice #3: Establish information processing systems that *deliver the right level of information to the right people at the right time* for the most effective and timely decision-making on a worldwide basis.

- Share information you gain - information relevant to increasing your productivity or effectiveness - with others in your organization who could benefit from it.
- Ensure that people you manage or work with abroad have the information they need to make as many local decisions as possible, in order to increase the quality of their decisions and to speed their response to local customer needs.

Practice #4: Track *global merger and acquisition activity and foreign investment patterns* of competitors and potential competitors.

- Conduct and update your competitive analysis on an ongoing basis to ensure that you are aware of what your key competitors are doing on a worldwide basis, even if some activities may seem unrelated to your current interests or priorities.
- Continually scan the global environment for potential competitors who could come from suppliers or customers and who might want to integrate vertically, as well as for diversified multinational corporations that might look to expand through merger and acquisition in your industry.

Practice #5: Monitor *international trade, tariff, economic, social and political changes* that may affect local, regional or international competitiveness.

- Read broadly in your industry and professional press and in less specialized literature about international social, political and economic megatrends.

Note: You will find a list of useful resources in Appendix A. The resources listed are of a general nature. You need to identify items specific to your industry and markets.

Source: Stephen H. Rhinesmith, *A Manager's Guide to Globalization: Six Keys to Success in a Changing World,* Homewood, IL: Business One Irwin, 1993 (Co-published with the American Society for Training and Development, Alexandria, VA).

IMPORTANT FACTORS IN THE INTERNATIONAL ENVIRONMENT

In conducting your environmental scan, you should seek to obtain and strategically use the following sets of information for each country/region that you are responsible for:

Economic Environment

Level of Economic Development
Population
Gross National Product
Per Capita Income
Literacy Level
Social Infrastructure
Natural Resources
Climate
Trade Unions
Membership in Regional Economic Blocs (E.C., L.A.F.T.A.)
Monetary and Fiscal Policies
Nature of Competition
Nature of Currency Convertibility
Inflation
Taxation System
Interest Rates
Wage and Salary Levels

Political Environment

Political Ideologies
Form of Government
Stability of Government
Strength of Opposition Parties and Interest Groups
Social Unrest
Political Strife and Insurgency
Governmental Attitude Towards Foreign Firms
Foreign Policy

Legal Environment

Legal Tradition
Effectiveness of Legal System
Treaties with Foreign Nations
Patent Trademark Laws
Laws Affecting Business Firms

Cultural Environment

Customs, Norms, Values, Beliefs
Languages
Attitudes
Social Institutions
Status Symbols
Religious Beliefs

GLOBAL BUSINESS THINKING: DEVELOPMENT PRIORITIES

After reviewing the material in **Module 1: Global Business Thinking**, describe what you consider to be your top three personal development priorities and those of your organization. For your personal development priorities, be as specific as you can be, e.g., description, action steps, and dates.

Development Priority #1	
Personal:	Organization:

Development Priority #2	
Personal:	Organization:

Development Priority #3	
Personal:	Organization:

NOTES

MODULE 2: CROSS-CULTURAL AWARENESS

Overview

Primary Objective: Recognize and examine familiar and unfamiliar cultural values, assumptions, and beliefs.

Units:

A: What Is Culture?

B: Developing Cultural Effectiveness

As a company moves onto the international playing field, culture comes to play an extremely important role in business success.

Culture is the code of behaviors, values, beliefs, and patterns of thinking that we learn as we grow and develop in our social groups. Culture determines how we view ourselves and others, how we behave, and how we perceive the world around us. We tend to believe that our way of seeing is the only way, or at least the best.

Although cultures can vary in dramatic ways, we can profile cultures according to their relationship to ten key variables: Nature, Time, Action, Communication, Space, Power, Individualism, Competitiveness, Structure, and Formality. These variables provide us with a frame of reference for understanding the characteristics of different cultures and adapting behaviors. The role of culture in doing business effectively becomes increasingly important as a company evolves into a global entity. Developing cultural effectiveness in business involves a three step process: Self- Awareness, Cross-Cultural Understanding, and Adapting Business Skills.

UNIT A: WHAT IS CULTURE?

Objectives

After completing this unit, you will be able to:

 Define the concept of 'culture.'

 Recognize key factors in the learning of culture.

 Identify ten key variables for profiling cultures.

CULTURE: A FRAME OF REFERENCE

Culture is the code of behaviors, values, beliefs, and patterns of thinking that we **learn** as we grow and develop in our social groups. Culture determines how we view ourselves and others, how we behave, and how we perceive the world around us. It distinguishes the members of one group of people from another.

The nucleus of each culture is built on core values. Values are **preferences** for certain states of affairs or outcomes over others.

A culture's core values are specific orientations to a number of key variables. All cultures face common basic problems, such as ways of relating to authority, dealing with conflict, and relating the individual to society.

To provide you with a simple **frame of reference** for profiling a culture and understanding its major characteristics, we focus on orientations to ten major variables*:

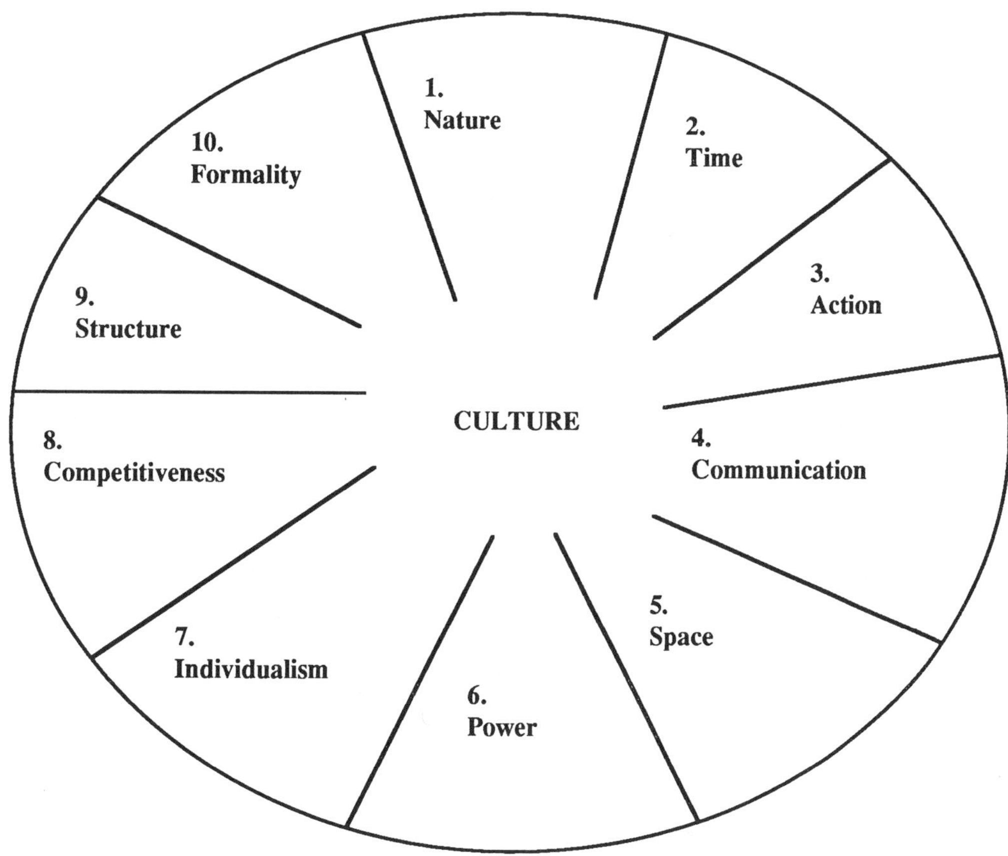

* These variables are adapted from the work of several anthropologists and international business consultants including: Geert Hofstede, Edward T. Hall, A. L. Kroeber, Clyde Kluckhohn, Florence Kluckhohn, Frederick Strodtbeck, Stephen H. Rhinesmith, and Nancy Adler.

PROFILING "CULTURE X"

Given the ten major variables, let's look at the core values of an imaginary culture called CULTURE X.

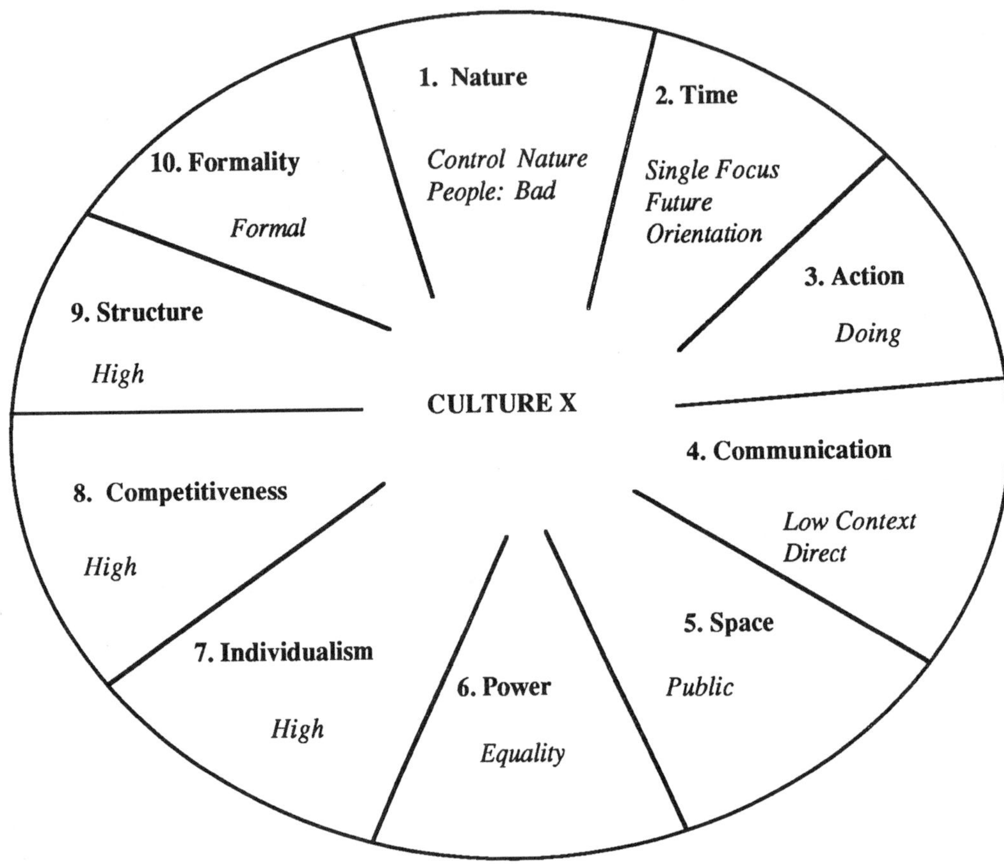

The core values or preferences of CULTURE X are:

1. The physical environment is to be controlled. Human nature is basically "bad."
2. The people of CULTURE X focus on one task or issue at a time and are primarily interested in the future rather than the present or the past.
3. Activity and accomplishment are valued over experience (being).
4. Talk is explicit and direct, and communication depends heavily on words rather than body language or tone.
5. The emphasis is placed on public as opposed to private space.
6. There is little tolerance for hierarchy.
7. Emphasis is placed on the individual rather than the group.
8. CULTURE X is aggressively competitive with a high value placed on achievement and success.
9. People in this culture do not like uncertainty. They create structure and networks to minimize ambiguity.
10. Relationships are primarily formal.

LEARNING CULTURE: INDIVIDUAL FACTORS

Before looking at the key variables in depth, it is important to understand that very few people belong to only one social group. An individual's cultural profile is not only shaped by national culture, but also by other factors such as: **family, region, neighborhood, education, profession, corporate culture, social class, gender, race, generation, religion, cultural heroes, and even other cultures.** Imagine a person in CULTURE X called Ms. Y. Ms. Y's family, neighborhood, corporate culture and social class stress Hierarchy rather than Equality, the Past rather than the Future, and Being rather than Doing. Ms. Y's personal culture profile will look more like the following:

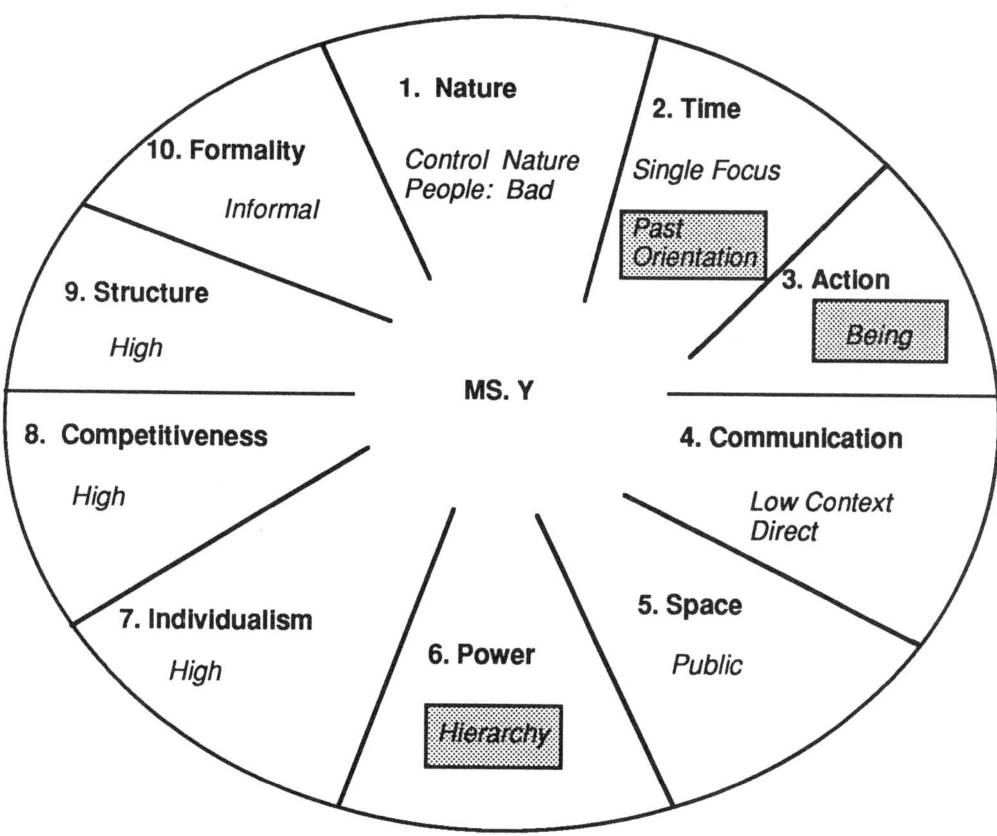

What do we learn from this? **We cannot make too many assumptions about a person from another culture. We may know a culture's core values very well, but an individual may be somewhat different. We need to pay attention, listen and observe.**

Let's look now at each of the ten variables.

NATURE

Different cultures approach nature (both the environment and human nature) from varied perspectives.

Definition

Environment

Cultures may believe that they:

- Have control over nature; that it should be changed to fit human needs.
- Should live in harmony with nature.
- Are controlled by nature.

Human Nature

Cultures may believe that:

- People are basically "good."
- People are basically "bad."
- People are a mixture of "good" and "bad."

Implications At Work

Environment

- Control over nature:
  - Organizational and business environments can be controlled.
  - The challenge is to engineer the environment to achieve goals.
- Harmony:
  - Decision making should facilitate harmonious relationships with nature and others.
  - Security and lifetime employment can have high value.
- Controlled by:
  - Presumptuous to claim direct control over plans, schedules, goals.

Human Nature

- Good:
  - Put right person in right job and empower him or her to perform.
- Bad:
  - Emphasis on control and monitoring of personnel.

NATURE (Cont'd)

Implications At Work

Human Nature (Cont'd)

- Good and Bad:
  - Personal development is possible.
  - Investment in training and professional development is desirable.

Illustrations

- Most North Americans believe that people can master nature. The harmony orientation can be observed in many Asian and American Indian cultures. The belief in the subjugation of individuals by nature can be seen in societies that place a high belief in fate, such as many Middle Eastern and Latin American societies.
- In the United States, there is a strong belief that human nature is basically good. There is an emphasis on directing one's destiny and perfecting one's self. Most other cultures believe that human nature is a mixture of good and evil.

Review Question 8:

How would you describe your own cultural orientation to nature?

Environment

Control Nature ________________ *Harmony with Nature* ________________ *Controlled by Nature*

Human Nature

Good ________________ *Mixed* ________________ *Bad*

TIME

A culture's use of time can communicate differences more profoundly than words.

Definition

In terms of time, cultures gravitate towards one of two types:

Single Focus
High concentration on one task or issue at a time with a commitment to schedules.

Multi-Focused
Greater emphasis on multiple tasks with concentration on relationship building rather than deadlines.

Cultures can also be categorized according to their orientation to the past, present, and future:

Past
High value placed on continuance of traditions.

Present
Short-term orientation aimed at quick results.

Future
Willingness to trade short-term gains for long-term results.

Implications At Work

Single Focus

- One thing done at a time.
- Deadlines, schedules taken seriously.
- Punctuality valued.
- Tasks central.
- Plans followed.

Multi-Focused

- Several things done at once.
- Commitments taken lightly.
- People almost always late.
- Relationships central.
- Plans changed frequently.

Past

- Changes and plans judged according to their fit with history and customs.

Present

- Changes and plans judged on fast payoff.

Future

- Changes and plans judged on expected future benefit.

TIME (Cont'd)

Illustrations

- In general, North Americans and northern Europeans are single-focus. Southern Europeans, Middle Easterners and Latin Americans tend to be multi-focused. The Japanese have elements of both styles, i.e., they are multi-focused regarding space (share office space) but demonstrate a single focus in appointments and schedules.
- Most North Americans are oriented to the present and the short-term future. East Asian cultures, in general, are both past- and future-oriented, i.e., they emphasize the goals and traditions of the past as well as long-term plans for the future. Middle Eastern cultures tend to be strongly rooted in traditions and customs of the past, while Latin American societies honor past traditions yet are present-oriented. European cultures honor tradition; however, they also display a future orientation. In general, European business plans for the future are longer term than those of the U.S. but shorter than those of Asia.

Review Question 9:

How would you describe your own cultural orientation to time?

Single Focus ____ *Multi-Focus*

Past ____________________ *Present* ____________________ *Future*

ACTION

Cultures, like individuals, can be oriented towards activity or passivity.

Definition

Doing Cultures
Stress is placed on action and accomplishments, achieving personal goals and improving standards of living.

Being Cultures
Stress is placed on working for the moment, release from stress, and experience rather than accomplishment.

Implications At Work

Doing
- Follow external standards of measurement.
- Motivate by promotions, raises, bonuses, recognition.

Being
- Put emphasis on job satisfaction.
- Cannot motivate by promises of future rewards.

Illustrations

- The U.S. is, arguably, the most action-oriented culture in the world; there is primary emphasis on doing and achieving measurable accomplishments. East Asian cultures tend to display "doing" and "being" orientations simultaneously, in that there is emphasis both on working very hard and on having a personal identity apart from one's tasks.
- A strong "being" orientation is observed in the Middle East and Latin America.
- Also, in many European countries, there is a "being" orientation in that the worth of a person is based more on character than accomplishments.

Review Question 10:

How would you describe your own cultural orientation to action?

Doing ____ *Being*

COMMUNICATION

A culture's orientation to communication is often very subtle. Thus, differences in communication style can cause a multitude of problems in sales, negotiations, and people management.

Definition

In terms of communication, cultures can be broadly classified into two categories:

Low Context
Information is given primarily in words; meaning is expressed explicitly.

High Context
Information is transmitted not just in words but also through a variety of contexts, such as voice tone, body language, facial expressions, eye contact, speech patterns, use of silence, past interactions, status, common friends, etc. The message in communications is more implicit.

Implications At Work

Low Context

- Message carried more by words than nonverbal signals.
- Communications are direct and seen as a means of exchanging information.
- Conflicts are depersonalized and work can proceed in the face of disagreement.
- Business relationships start and end more quickly and depend less on personal trust between individuals.
- One's identity tends to be more rooted in oneself and one' s accomplishments.
- Thought patterns are more compartmentalized and inductive.
- Specific instructions are given and information flows along formal lines of hierarchy.

High Context

- High use of nonverbal signals.
- Communications are indirect and seen as an art form.
- Conflicts must be resolved before work can progress.
- Business relationships depend on trust and build slowly.
- One's identity tends to be more rooted in groups.
- Thought patterns are holistic and deductive.
- Few rules are given and information is accessed through informal networks.

Illustrations

- The U.S., Germany, Switzerland and Scandinavia are low context.
- Asian, Latin and Middle Eastern countries are high context.
- Southern European countries are in between, i.e., "middle" context.

COMMUNICATION (Cont'd)

Review Question 11:

How would you describe your own cultural orientation to communication?

High context ———————————————— *Low Context*

SPACE

The use and meaning of space represent an important, but too often neglected, aspect of cultures.

Definition

Cultures can be categorized according to their distinctions between private and public spaces.

People in different cultures have contrasting needs in terms of their personal space requirements, i.e., distances between individuals, the degree to which physical space is demarcated public or private, and the rules governing the use of each type.

Implications At Work

Private

- Closed door meetings.
- Private offices and partitions.
- Minimal interruptions and disruption.
- Permission needed to enter private space.

Public

- Large rooms, few if any partitions.
- Managers interspersed with employees.

Illustrations

- Standards for distance vary across cultures; for example, a comfortable social distance for Latin Americans or Arabs would be roughly equivalant to a personal or intimate distance for Americans. In Scandinavia or Germany, however, an American businessperson might feel that the distance appropriate for conducting business is a little *too* distant.

- The location and size of an office do not provide a universal indicator of the importance of its occupant. For example, the offices of French and Japanese supervisors are ordinarily found among those of their subordinates, as opposed to the corners of buildings or the upper floors, as is the case typically in the U.S. Arab, Latin American and many Asian executive offices – regarded as spacious by their standards – are considered crowded by Americans.

Review Question 12:

How would you describe your own cultural orientation to space?

Private ———————————————————— *Public*

POWER

The power variable demonstrates the extent to which the less powerful members of a society expect and accept that power is distributed unequally.

Definition

In some cultures inequality is a given. The culture satisfies a need for dependence and security.

In other countries, inequality is thought to be an unsatisfactory state of affairs. While it may be unavoidable, it is considered correct to minimize it through legal, political, and economic means.

Some Implications At Work

Hierarchy

- Levels of power and authority are highly demarcated.
- Employees accept that the manager has a right to more power than they do.
- Employees do work only in the way the manager requires of them.
- No work bypasses the chain of authority.
- Negotiators must command respect by their title and status.

Equality

- The organization is flatter.
- Employees do not accept that the manager has an inherent right to greater power; it must be earned.
- Employees do their work in what they believe is the most appropriate way.
- Work regularly bypasses the manager.
- Title, status, and formal position have less influence in negotiations.

Illustrations

- Arab, most Latin American, and East Asian countries accept hierarchy. The exceptions include Argentina and Costa Rica, which are strongly European-influenced. Also, France, Belgium, Spain, and Turkey have a high tolerance for inequality.
- Countries that value equality include the U.S., the U.K., Ireland, Australia, and New Zealand.

Review Question 13:

How would you describe your own cultural orientation to power?

Hierarchy ———————————————————— *Equality*

INDIVIDUALISM

Individualism shows the extent to which countries elevate the role of the individual over the role of the group.

Definition

Individualism characterizes those cultures in which the bonds between individual members are relatively loose; people are independent and expected to take care of themselves or, at most, the nuclear family. Guilt and fear of loss of self-respect are central to social control.

Collectivism characterizes those cultures in which individual interests are subordinate to group interests. Cohesive groups protect their members in exchange for loyalty and obedience. Social control is based upon the fear of losing face and the possibility of shame.

When individualism is valued, the "I" predominates over the "We." Individual identity is key and speaking one's mind is a sign of honesty. Laws and rights are the same for everyone and political power is exercised by individual voters.

When individualism is not highly valued, identity is based on the social network to which the person belongs. Harmony, rather than speaking one's mind, is a key value. Laws and rights differ by group and political power is wielded by interest groups. The in-group expects loyalty in exchange for security and protection.

Some Implications At Work

Individualism

- Motivation tends towards achievement and power.
- Tasks are valued over relationships.
- Conflict is seen as inevitable.
- Management entails management of individuals.
- Hiring and promotion are based on skill and roles.
- Employer-employee relationship is based on mutual advantage.

Collectivism

- Motivation tends towards affiliation.
- Relationships are valued over the task.
- Conflict is seen as a negative force.
- Management entails management of groups.
- Hiring and promotion takes in-group into account.
- Employer-employee relationship is like a family connection.

INDIVIDUALISM (Cont'd)

Illustrations

- Countries with a low value in regard to individualism include most Asian, Arab and Latin American countries. One exception is Brazil, which is a highly individualistic country.
- Countries with a high value in regard to individualism include most Northern European countries, Australia, New Zealand, Canada and the U.S.A. Finland and Germany, however, are the lowest-ranking in individualism in Northern Europe.
- In Southern Europe, Portugal and Greece are low in individualism; Spain is relatively low; and Italy is relatively high.

Review Question 14:

How would you describe your own cultural orientation to individualism?

Individualism ______________________________ *Collectivism*

COMPETITIVENESS

The competitiveness variable demonstrates the degree to which achievement and success dominate over caring for others and the quality of life.

Definition

Competitiveness characterizes cultures in which achievement, assertiveness, and competition are reinforced. Social and gender roles tend to be distinct. Men are expected to be assertive, tough and driven by material success. Women, on the other hand, are expected to be modest, nurturing, and concerned primarily with the quality of life. In many western industrialized societies, this distinction between the sex roles is diminishing.

Cooperativeness characterizes cultures in which social and gender roles overlap. Everyone is expected to demonstrate modesty, nurturing, and a concern for the quality of life.

When competitiveness is valued, the culture is predominantly materialistic, with an emphasis on assertiveness and the acquisition of money, property, goods, etc. High value is placed on ambition, decisiveness, performance, speed, and size. One lives to work.

When cooperation is valued, stress is placed on the quality of life, sympathy, nurturing, and relationships. One works to live. High value is placed on consensus and intuition.

Some Implications At Work

Competitiveness

- Money acts as a motivator.
- High concern with achievement and performance.

Cooperativeness

- Money less of a motivator.
- High concern with job satisfaction.

Illustrations

- It is very difficult, with this cultural dimension, to group the major world regions. It is important, therefore, to look at each country on an individual basis.
- The U.S., Great Britain, New Zealand, Australia, Japan, the Philippines, Hong Kong, Germany, Switzerland, Belgium, Greece, Italy and some Latin countries (such as Venezuela, Mexico, Ecuador, Colombia and Argentina) are competitive cultures.

COMPETITIVENESS (Cont'd)

Illustrations

- Canada ranks only moderately high in competitiveness.
- Latin countries that do not place a high value on competitiveness include: Spain, Panama, Chile, Costa Rica, Guatemala, Peru, and Uruguay.
- Other low-competitive, or high cooperative, countries include the majority of Asian and Scandinavian countries and some countries of Northern European including: Denmark, The Netherlands, and France.
- Arab countries are midway between competitive and cooperative cultures.

Review Question 15:

How would you describe your own cultural orientation to competitiveness?

Competitiveness ______________________________ *Cooperativeness*

STRUCTURE

Structure tells us the extent to which the members of a culture experience threat or discomfort by uncertainty or unknown situations.

Definition

Structure is expressed as a need for predictability and rules, written and unwritten.

Cultures that value structure seek to reduce ambiguity and make events predictable and interpretable. Conflict is threatening and there is a perceived need for rules and regulations. Anxiety and stress are high. A need for structure should not be confused, however, with an aversion to risk. Reducing ambiguity may require risk.

Cultures with low structure needs are more tolerant of unknown situations, people, and ideas. Anxiety levels are lower and tolerance of deviance is higher. Dissent is acceptable.

Some Implications At Work

High Structure

- Lifetime employment valued.
- Need for clear roles and responsibilities.
- Stress on avoiding failure.
- Inner drive to work hard.

Low Structure

- High job mobility.
- Loose role and responsibility definitions.
- Willingness to take risks.
- Hard work not a virtue in its own right.

Illustrations

- Countries that place a high value on structure include Latin, Islamic, Mediterranean, German-speaking and some Asian countries (Japan, South Korea, Taiwan and Thailand).

- Countries that place a relatively low value on structure include: Southeast Asia (Hong Kong, Indonesia, India, Malaysia, the Philippines and Singapore), the U.S.A., the U.K., Ireland, Canada, Australia and New Zealand, and Scandinavian countries, as well as the Netherlands.

Review Question 16:

How would you describe your own cultural orientation to structure?

High Structure ________________________________ *Low Structure*

FORMALITY

Formality refers to the importance placed on the existence of and adherence to rules for acceptable self-presentation and business/social behavior.

Definition

Formal cultures place high emphasis on following business protocol and social customs. People from informal cultures feel more comfortable dispensing with ceremony and conducting business more casually.

Implications At Work

Formal Cultures

- Tend to have a strong sense of history, culture and tradition.
- Are more mindful of the past.
- Tend to be more class or hierarchy conscious and have a stronger sense of social position.
- Display greater attention to observing protocol regarding rank and hierarchy.
- Have greater respect for rules – rules are made to be observed and preserved.
- Feel that visitors should observe decorum to show sincerity and seriousness in doing business.
- Establish trust in business more on social acceptance and relationships, in general.
- Have customs and/or rituals regarding appropriate dress, greetings, business card exchange, forms of address, scheduling and conducting meetings, communication styles (verbal and nonverbal), eating and drinking, entertaining and gift giving.
- Tend to form relationships more slowly, but, once formed, relationships are deeper and more permanent.

Informal Cultures

- Tend not to have deeply ingrained traditions or a strong sense of historical continuity.
- Have high regard for change and view progress as more important than preserving customs.
- Are casual, relaxed and friendly when doing business.
- Feel uncomfortable with wide social or power disparities.
- Tend to have more direct and candid communication styles.
- Can place more emphasis on observance of schedules or deadlines than image, status or relationships.
- Tend not to see the formation of a good relationship as a pre-requisite for doing business.
- Display informal manners in nearly all aspects of business and socializing.

FORMALITY (Cont'd)

Illustrations

- The United States and Australia are widely considered to be the two most informal cultures in the world.
- Canada and New Zealand are fairly informal, but more formal than the U.S. or Australia.
- Latin American, Arab, Asian and European cultures are all formal. The specific customs, however, vary greatly by region, and also by country within the region.

Review Question 17:

How would you describe your own cultural orientation to formality?

Formal ———————————————————— *Informal*

REINVENTING THE WHEEL

There's an old taboo against reinventing the wheel. But, there are **wheels** and then there are *wheels*!

Our ***wheel*** presents the variables to be used when you want to profile an unfamiliar culture or when you are about to confront a cross-cultural situation. It provides you with a starting point for asking questions about a new culture and how to adapt your business style. For example, "Will my typical informality be appropriate?" Can I expect the individual with whom I meet to make a quick decision? Will my direct, explicit style of communication be effective? These types of questions will help you prepare, and good preparation is at the heart of cross-cultural effectiveness.

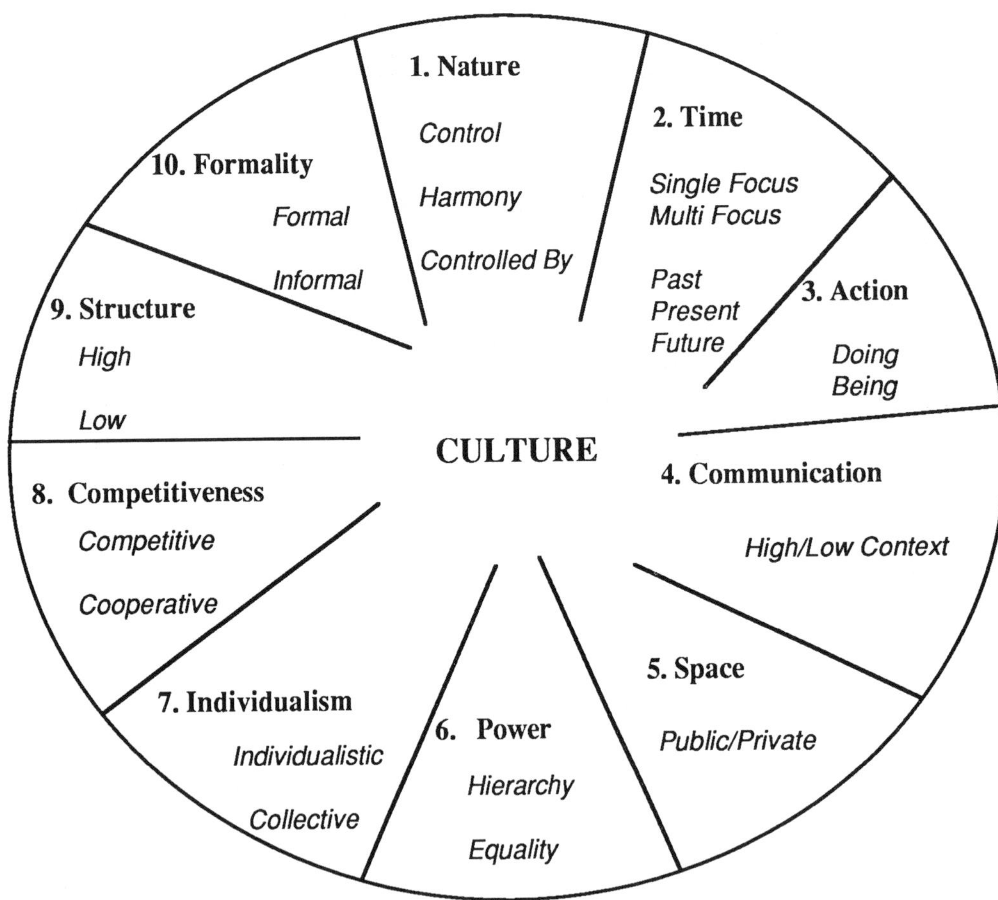

Refer to this wheel as you consider the Study Questions on the following pages.

CULTURAL VARIABLES AT WORK

Now that you have studied our ten cultural variables, review the following critical incidents and determine which key variables are at work. Make notes on each incident and explain the differing value orientations of the involved parties.

In the remainder of the program, you will be applying your knowledge of these variables to a range of cross-cultural business interactions. You will find suggested answers in Appendix D on pages D2-D3.

Study Question 1:
What cultural variables are at work in this incident?

Andrew Crowley, a Marketing Development Manager, was having some problems communicating with his Italian counterpart, Alberto Monti. Deciding that voice mail and electronic mail were probably not sufficient to establish the kind of relationship needed for truly effective communications, Andrew scheduled a trip to Naples to meet Alberto face-to-face and discuss several important issues regarding the launch of a new consumer product.

After he scheduled his trip, however, it occurred to Andrew that, since he was going to be in Europe, he should take advantage of it and plan other visits to meet with some of his counterparts in Paris, Brussels and Madrid. He scheduled a one-week itinerary.

Upon arriving in Italy, he first met with an expatriate Director, Ned Turner. Ned commended him for coming and suggested that, in addition to working out some details regarding the launch, he spend time getting to know Alberto and other members of the team personally and enjoying his visit and the Italians' hospitality.

Andrew tried to take Ned's advice and changed his plans when it became clear that two days would not be sufficient to accommodate all the discussions, long meals and entertainment that Alberto had planned. On the fourth day, however, even though he had not gotten as far on the project as he had hoped, he was ready to leave on the first available plane.

Andrew nearly lost his patience when Ned suggested that he delay his departure for one more day in order to meet and get to know some other members of the launch team in Italy who had just flown in from a conference. Instead, though, Andrew held his tongue and gritted his teeth at the prospect of sitting through another three-hour lunch.

Your answer:

CULTURAL VARIABLES AT WORK

Study Question 2:
What cultural variables are at work in this incident?

A manufacturing plant in Thailand was falling behind schedule in producing semiconductors for worldwide distribution. To investigate the reasons behind this lag, Operations and Manufacturing managers Cathy Hutchison and Sean Forlani set up a conference call with the Thai managers in charge of production, assembly and testing.

Cathy started by asking them for feedback on the constraints in the factory contributing to the fallback on the shipping schedule. There was silence and then one of the Thais asked if they could please hold. Cathy and Sean held on the line for 10 minutes, hearing a discussion in Thai in the background. When the Thais got back on the line, the assembly manager said, "Yes, there were quality control problems but that they were working very hard to resolve them as soon as possible." Wanting the specifics, Sean began asking a series of questions to uncover more detailed information. However, the answers he received were, in his opinion, insufficient.

Finally, Cathy asked if there were constraints in the assembly. The assembly manager answered, "Yes, there are." Relieved, Sean asked how long it would take to fix the problem. There was a long pause, so Sean then asked if they could fix it in a week. The Thais said they could. Cathy then asked for the maximum number of devices that they could commit to shipping out each day, after the week had passed. The Thais agreed on a number. Sean and Cathy ended the phone call feeling satisfied that everything had been taken care of and was under control.

In two weeks, however, although the assembly problem had been fixed and the factory workers were working significant overtime hours, the plant was not meeting the quota per day that had been agreed upon. Exasperated, Sean and Cathy set up another conference call to ask the Thais what was the matter and why. Again, the Thais put them on hold and then continued to answer in general terms. Finally, Sean asked if they had found constraints in any other areas besides assembly. The manager in charge of testing then answered that the primary constraint had been in the testing area and that they had just about resolved it. Angrily, Sean asked why he hadn't told them about the problem before. There was a long pause and then the production manager said, "Last time, you asked about assembly and we did tell you." Sean and Cathy terminated the phone call shortly thereafter, wondering if the Thais were lazy, prone to hiding things, or just couldn't understand English.

Your answer:

CULTURAL VARIABLES AT WORK

Study Question 3:
What cultural variables are at work in this incident?

John Anderson, a Manager in Corporate Training, was recently promoted to handle all education and training for the European region. The company's Training Center in Europe had folded two years earlier, after being in operation for only one year, and – although a little scared – John looked forward to the challenge of successfully relaunching training in Europe.

As the first step, John established contact with the 16 European Managing Directors and with their help over a period of months, worked out a competency-based curriculum of training courses. It was hectic for a while – John often felt as though he was making it all up as he was going along – but the curriculum was finally established and the Center was ready again for the first pilot program.

Everything seemed okay – except for his relationship with Etienne Horville, the French Managing Director. The other Managing Directors – particularly those from Scandinavia and the U.K. – had shown appreciation for his efforts, given him lots of helpful tips, and even shown a sense of humor regarding the overall scanty procedures given John by his superiors.

Monsieur Horville, however, was often combative, debating the viability of John's plans and referring frequently to the failed efforts of the old Training Center. He also kept pressing for more time to conduct needs assessment and job analysis studies prior to the curriculum design phase and, once the design was finalized, he questioned its relevancy to the French office.

Three weeks before the first pilot, John was concerned about the total lack of registration from the French office and called Monsieur Horville. The executive assistant said that Monsieur Horville was in a meeting. Very concerned, John asked the assistant a few questions to try to ascertain the level of interest in the office in the pilot program and find out what, if any, marketing had been done. The next day, when the Director returned John's phone call, he coldly informed him that no managers from the French office would be attending the pilot.

Your answer:

CULTURAL VARIABLES AT WORK

Study Question 4
What cultural variables are at work in this incident?

Joanna Adams is responsible for managing various aspects of business for several health care product lines internationally. Her most recent project included working with an affiliate company in the Netherlands to prepare a media campaign regarding a new health care product to be launched. This was a very important and urgent project, as a rival competitor was about to launch a similar product and the pressure was on to get the product and the advertising to market first.

Because time was so short, Joanna was putting in extremely long hours at the office, coming in at 6:00 a.m. to begin communicating by telephone with the Netherlands team and leaving at 8:00 p.m. regularly. Her staff team in the U.S. were also working very hard.

Joanna was beginning to resent her Dutch counterpart and P.R. staff, who were not, to her mind, pulling their weight on the project. To meet the project deadlines, they needed to put in a lot of overtime as well. Finally, one morning at 11:00 a.m. (EST), while toiling over some focus group reports, she gave her counterpart, Hans Van Meer, a call. She was enraged to find out that he had already left the office, and she vowed to call her superior the next morning.

Your answer:

UNIT B: DEVELOPING CROSS-CULTURAL EFFECTIVENESS

Objectives

After completing this unit, you will be able to:

 Recognize typical reactions to experiencing a new culture.

 Distinguish between the "seen" and "unseen" aspects of culture.

 Identify a three-step process for developing cultural effectiveness.

 Understand the concept of ethnocentrism.

 Identify important personal attributes for cross-cultural effectiveness.

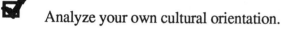

 Analyze your own cultural orientation.

 Analyze the major characteristics of another culture.

THE "FEEL" OF CULTURE

We take our own culture for granted. It is like the air we breathe; it is simply *there* as a part of who we are.

If you have ever visited another country, you know that cultural differences are a large part of the **fun** and **fear** of foreign travel. For the first time, you may become conscious of your own cultural background, as well as that of others.

- You may step out of the hotel and the language is incomprehensible to you.
- People are making gestures to one another in the street, but you don't know what the gestures mean.
- You stand out in the crowd because you are dressed differently.
- The food looks strange to your eyes and feels strange on your tongue.
- When you meet with people, they stand very close to you and make you feel uncomfortable.
- The people are never punctual at meetings you've arranged.
- When you do meet, they seem to spend a long time making what you consider to be "small talk" before getting down to business.

You are experiencing another culture and you may feel:

DISORIENTED	FRUSTRATED
NOT IN CONTROL	CURIOUS
DEPRESSED	EXCITED
AGGRESSIVE	DISAPPOINTED
RESENTFUL	ALONE
SUPERIOR	HOMESICK
INFERIOR	BORED
WITHDRAWN	AFRAID
INSECURE	DEFENSIVE

AND MORE!

CULTURE: ON-STAGE AND BACKSTAGE

Culture is rather like a theatrical show. There are parts you see and parts you don't. On-stage, you may see the actors, hear their lines, watch the action, but backstage there is much more supporting activity. What you see, hear, smell, taste, and touch is only a small portion of what is actually happening. This can be why it's often difficult to explain what is *specifically* making you feel uncomfortable or frustrated.

You can also think about culture as an iceberg. Two-thirds is underwater (or backstage) while the other third is on the surface (on-stage).

ON-STAGE	BACKSTAGE	
Music	Conceptions of:	Approaches to:
Literature	Self	Work
Painting and Sculpture	Raising Children	Revealing Problems
Theater	Relating to Nature	Solving Problems
Dance	Beauty	Social Interaction
Food and Drink	Truth	Decision Making
Clothes	Goodness	Communication
Greetings	Authority	Sex
Gestures	Sin	Deadlines
Gift Giving	Friendship	
Outward Behaviors	Fairness	
Manners	Time	
Rituals and Ceremonies	Space	
Myths and Legends	Leadership	
	Status	
	Responsibilities	
	Gender	

CULTURE: OURS IS BEST!

Given the feelings that experiencing a new culture can generate, it's no wonder we often fall into the trap of being ethnocentric, i.e., believe in the "inherent" superiority of our own group's culture.

Becoming aware of and sensitive to other cultures does not mean that we lose our own culture; we can never do that. Rather it means that we are able to respect differences and understand multiple frames of reference.

Hasty cultural evaluations are the international manager's worst enemy.

Avoid terms like:

"That doesn't make sense."

"That's stupid."

"Strange."

"Weird."

"Unbelievable."

"Dumb."

"Lazy."

"Bizarre."

"Devious."

"Sly."

"Rude."

Review Question 18:

Think about a situation in which you have felt that someone with whom you were dealing was acting in an ethnocentric way, i.e., putting you and your culture down. How did you feel? What was your immediate reaction? Can you recall situations in which you have acted in an ethnocentric manner?

EFFECTIVE PERSONAL ATTRIBUTES

You will become more cross-culturally effective if you can develop the following attributes.

When confronted with a new culture, try to:

- Set realistic expectations for yourself and others.
- Be curious about the new culture and seek to learn all you can. What are the patterns? What is the logic? What makes the other culture tick?
- Also look at events and experiences from the other person's point of view.
- Keep hold of your sense of humor. Don't let it go.
- Be tolerant of yourself and others.
- Accept that you're going to make mistakes.
- Be personable, without having to be liked by everyone.
- Keep an objective frame of mind and avoid blame.
- Build relationships over time and reach mutual understandings.
- Maintain confidence in your own abilities and strengths.
- Relax, don't rush. Take time to learn the rules of the culture.

Don't

- Keep evaluating the other culture in terms of "good," "bad," etc. Keep judgments to a minimum.
- Keep comparing the unfamiliar culture with your own.
- Deny that you may have problems. Recognize the emotions involved and move on to find appropriate solutions.
- Assume that deep-down we are all the same.

THREE STEPS TO CULTURAL EFFECTIVENESS

As well as developing personal attributes for working across cultures, you also need to sharpen your cultural analysis skills. From analyses of your own and the foreign culture, you need to adapt your business skills so they will be effective in the different working environment.

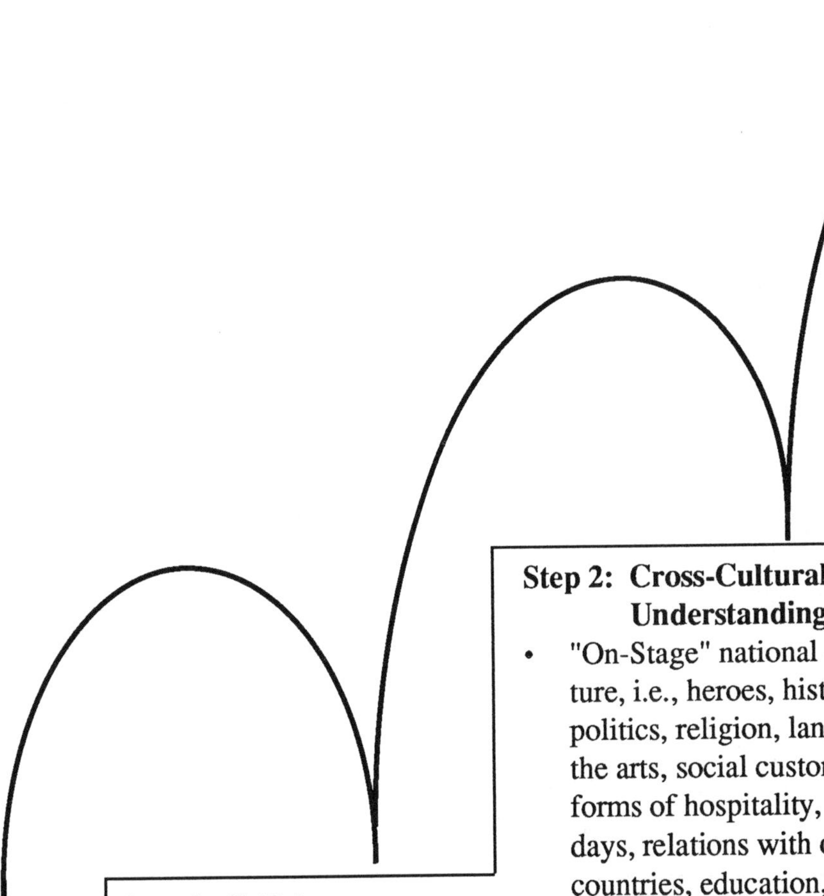

Step 1: Self-Awareness

- Your own culture
- Roles and behaviors as a member of your culture
- Attitudes, values and expectations towards such cultural variables as Nature, Time, Action, Communication, Space, Power, Individualism, Competitiveness, Structure, and Formality.

Step 2: Cross-Cultural Understanding

- "On-Stage" national culture, i.e., heroes, history, politics, religion, language, the arts, social customs, forms of hospitality, holidays, relations with other countries, education, etc.
- "On-Stage" business culture; i.e., greetings, topics of conversation, dress, entertaining, gift giving, protocol, business practices, do's and taboos, etc.
- "Backstage" culture, i.e., attitudes, values and expectations toward the cultural variables.

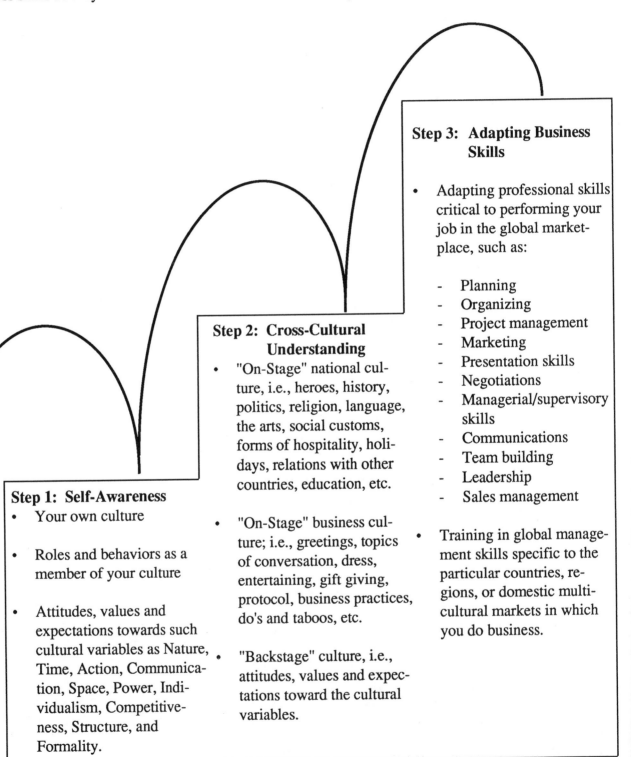

Step 3: Adapting Business Skills

- Adapting professional skills critical to performing your job in the global marketplace, such as:
  - Planning
  - Organizing
  - Project management
  - Marketing
  - Presentation skills
  - Negotiations
  - Managerial/supervisory skills
  - Communications
  - Team building
  - Leadership
  - Sales management
- Training in global management skills specific to the particular countries, regions, or domestic multicultural markets in which you do business.

STEP 1: SELF-AWARENESS

Knowing your own cultural preferences is the first step to becoming cross-culturally effective. In Unit A: What Is Culture?, you reviewed each of the ten variables and decided how you relate to each one.

Bring your decisions from Unit A and write them in the appropriate parts of the circle below.

You now have a "snapshot" of your cultural profile.

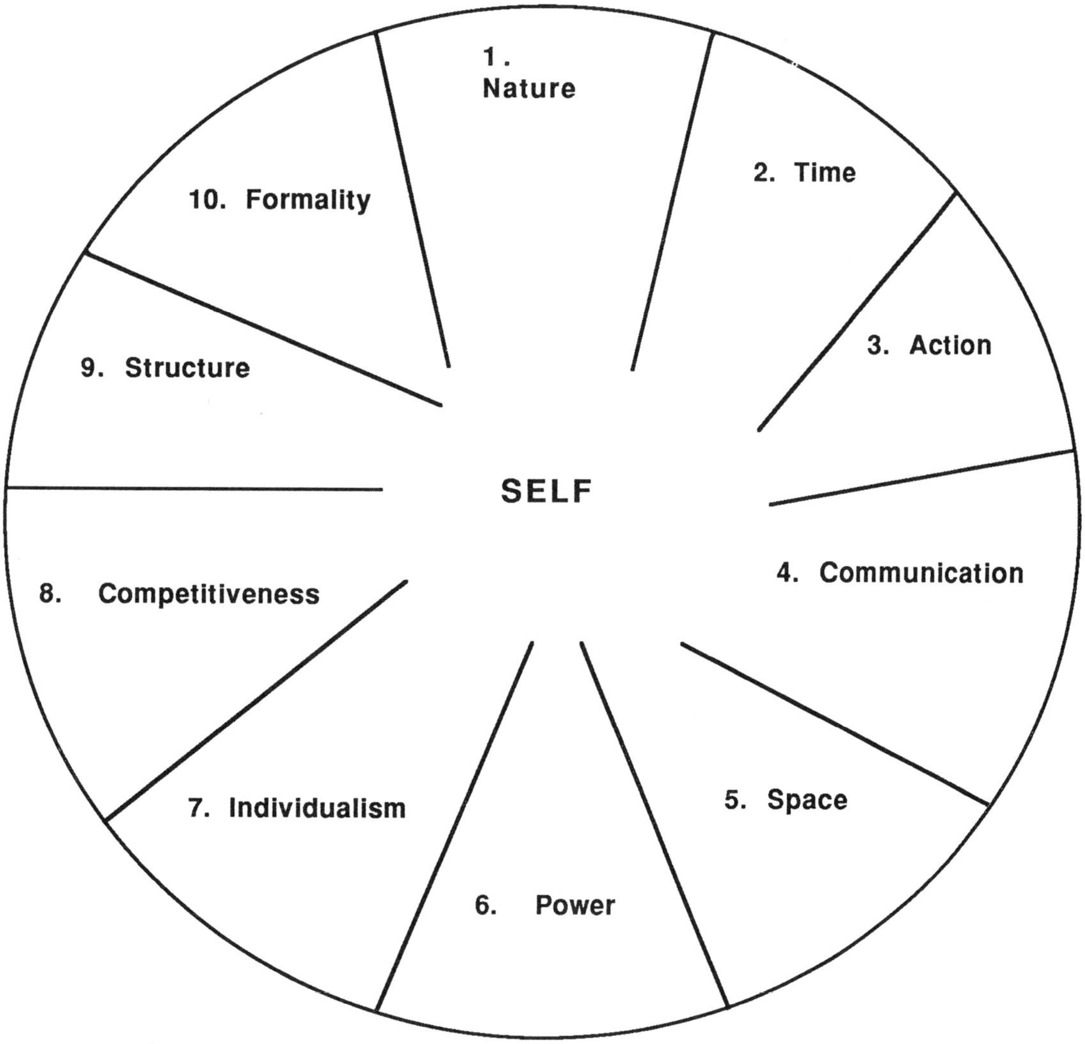

STEP 2: CROSS-CULTURAL UNDERSTANDING

Now that you have an understanding of your own cultural preferences, the next step is to analyze the preferences of the culture with which you are going to do business.

For this exercise, you will profile the key preferences of Japanese culture. To do this, read the scenario on the following pages. As you read, identify the key preferences related to Nature, Time, etc., and write your results in the circle below.

You will find suggested answers in Appendix D on pages D4-D6.

Study Question 5: What orientation does Japanese culture have to each of the ten cultural variables?

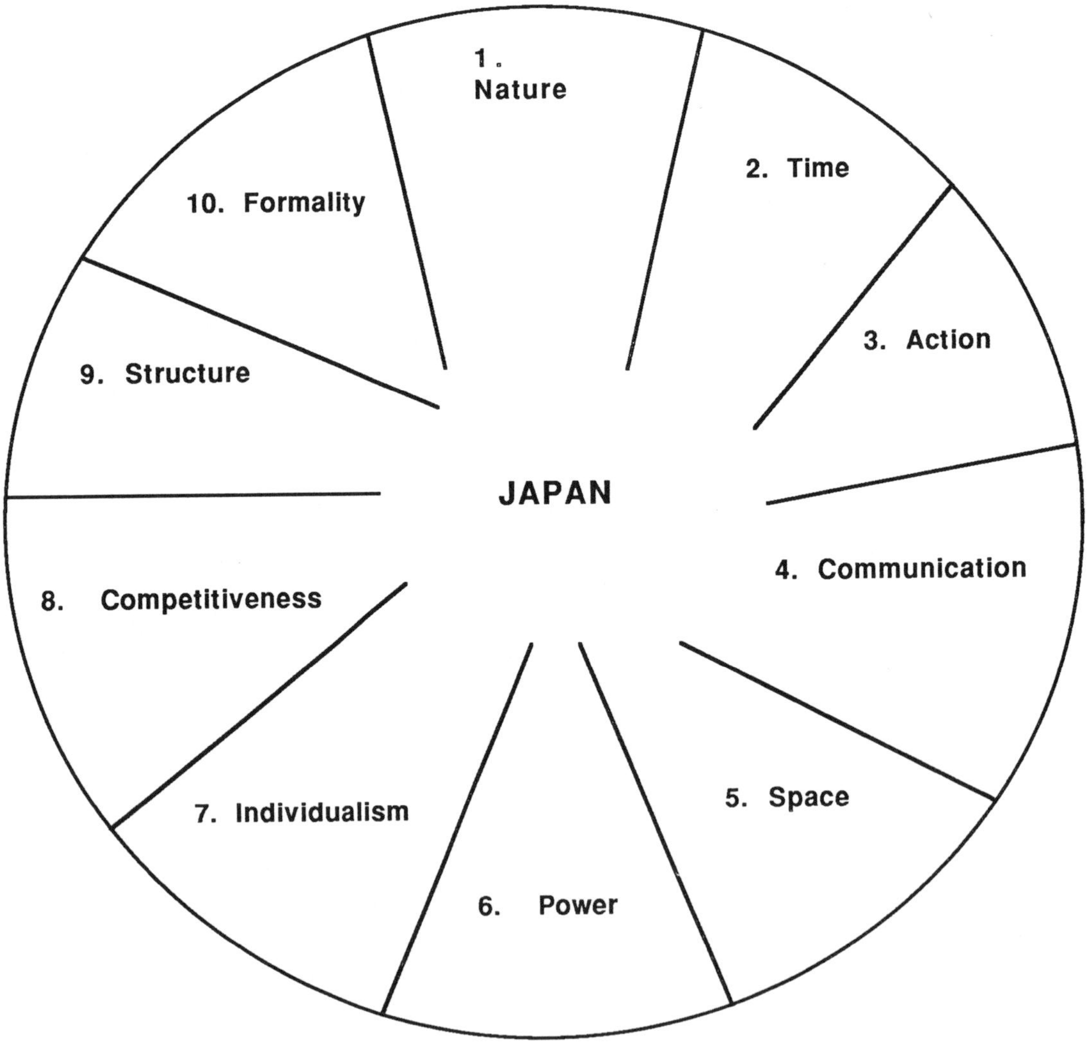

JAPAN

1. Nature

2. Time

3. Action

4. Communication

5. Space

6. Power

7. Individualism

8. Competitiveness

9. Structure

10. Formality

JAPANESE SCENARIO

You are currently serving as Director of Business Marketing in the international division of a major U.S. telecommunications firm. Most of your work involves expanding the firm's international marketing capability through joint ventures, alliances, and investments.

One of your recent projects is the formation of a joint venture fiber-optic communications company – OFC Co. Ltd. – with five Japanese companies. Of these five, however, the primary partner is the optical fiber communications subsidiary of a major Japanese firm, Hibiya Corp. The mission of the newly-created OFC is to manufacture, sell and service digital transmission equipment for public and private network customers in Japan.

The majority of OFC resources will – at least for the first few years – be provided by the Hibiya subsidiary; your division has agreed to provide capital, share technology, and participate in the leadership and management of the joint-venture company.

The first phase of formal negotiations is now complete and, on the whole, it proceeded rather smoothly. The output was the ceremonial signing of a contract with the Chairman of Hibiya to form OFC. The three principals with whom you communicated the most during these negotiations were the General Manager, President and Executive Vice President of the subsidiary. Prior to entering the first phase, you made sure to learn as much as you could about the Japanese, especially in regard to business and social etiquette. Your homework served you well throughout the stages of business card exchange, gift giving, entertaining, consensus building, etc. — and you even enjoyed the chance to learn experientially about the protocol of a different culture.

However, in the second phase – contract implementation and further negotiation – you have been encountering some problems. Negotiations have been stretching on for months regarding the details of the joint roles of your company and Hibiya in OFC operations, to a large extent because subsequent talks have involved entirely new sets of people. Different section chiefs have been pulled in and out of the negotiations according to the issues being discussed. After spending so much time on relationship- and trust-building in phase one, you had hoped to move on immediately to implementation; however, this obviously is not going to be the case. You have tried to be patient throughout this lengthy decision making process, but you are under pressure from your management to get OFC fully operational, up to U.S. standards, and making a profit within the next five years.

The President of your division has requested that your upcoming trip to the OFC facilities in Tokyo be extended and include an audit of the primary functions of the joint-venture company. You have politely informed the General Manager (Konosuke Watanabe, with whom you have developed a good relationship) of the reasons for your trip. He has responded by arranging for you to visit extensively with the following section chiefs in order to observe the processes at work in their departments:

- Masami Ogiso, Section Chief, Production
- Tadashi Kawaguchi, Section Chief, Marketing
- Kenichi Ishihara, Section Chief, Sales
- Shojiro Atarashi, Section Chief, Personnel
- Hideo Suzuki, Section Chief, Control and Finance

Your plan for the first part of the trip is to continue to develop relationships with the section chiefs and observe operations. Then, during the latter part, you will set forth your observations and recommendations for improvement both within the quality circle meetings held by each section and in individual meetings with the section heads. With the Japanese concern for quality (which you certainly have seen at work so far), you figure that, if you position any changes in the context of continuous improvement, you will not encounter resistance.

JAPANESE SCENARIO (Cont'd)

After several weeks in Tokyo, however, you have begun the process of improvement recommendations – and have not been meeting with much success at all. Instead of welcoming your suggestions, the Japanese have been responding either with silence, reluctance to take action, or talk of "further discussions." This has been very frustrating, as your recommendations would only serve to make operations and organizational interfaces more efficient and/or effective. You are seriously beginning to question whether or not this alliance will work. The project is a *joint* venture; your division is not just pouring money and technology into Hibiya as an investment. You thought it was agreed that leadership and management would be shared; now, you are unsure as to whether the Japanese ever really came to terms with that part of the agreement.

The issues you have brought up so far (and reactions to them) include the following:

- In regard to production, the two key items that you have surfaced are:
  - **The need for communication linkages between OFC in Japan and the U.S. division in regard to equipment orders.** For you to discharge your responsibilities back home, you need to be able to access information on customer orders and production on a day-to-day basis. However, when you talked with Ogiso-san and several of his team members regarding the possibility of your division's providing them with some of the latest data communications equipment, you were met with blank stares. When you went on to explain that this change would allow them to update their old system free-of-charge, you were confronted with a very long period of silence.
  - **The need for increasing manufacturing output, so as to meet projected orders.** You know, however, that your division cannot afford to give funds for hiring additional personnel and that Hibiya probably cannot either. Your idea was to increase output without further staffing by introducing robotized steps at several key points in the assembly. In fact, not only would this make production more efficient, but it would also slightly reduce staffing needs. This would be an excellent opportunity for the Japanese to lay off several less-than-productive manufacturing personnel. On the production floor, you could not help but notice that several of the teams contained workers who, in your opinion, were a little slower than the rest and needed to be "covered" for by the faster team members. In speaking with Ogiso-san and Atarashi-san about this, you were met with vague responses about "the importance of teamwork throughout the process." You were not sure as to their real reactions to your proposal and wondered what part of your recommendation was displeasing to them and why.
- In regard to marketing, the issue of strategy has proven unsettling. A major objective of this visit was for you to work closely with Kawaguchi-san to develop market strategy and integrate the strategy more fully with the sales effort. When you asked to see a sample of a marketing plan, you were met with a polite "I will try" phrase. One week later, no plan was forthcoming. You decided, in a marketing section meeting you attended, to:
  - outline the importance of a written market plan as a part of the overall business plan,
  - communicate the demands on you for presenting a marketing strategy to the head of your division in two months, and
  - show your respect for the Japanese marketing team by inviting them to submit their ideas directly to you in regard to all aspects of expanding OFC's business.

  The day afterward, your friend, the General Manager, invited you out to dinner. Pleased to have his company for an evening, you were surprised when, over drinks, he politely informed you, "Marketing is not done in Japan as it is in the West." Wondering if he was trying to communicate to you that you had been out of line in some way in the marketing meeting, you pressed him to

JAPANESE SCENARIO (Cont'd)

explain exactly how it was different. However, he did not answer in clear terms but stated that Kawaguchi-san and his staff have very strong technical and engineering backgrounds and are very qualified to handle marketing.

- In regard to sales, you have been particularly watchful. Prior to your trip, you sought advice from several U.S. executives who had been involved in joint ventures with Japanese companies, and the sales function kept coming up as an area with high potential for failure. In fact, they all recommended putting in an expatriate sales manager to work alongside the Japanese salesforce manager.

  You have had many discussions with Ishihara-san and he has been most kind in allowing you to examine his department's workings fully. You have found that:

  – The sales function is not as delineated from other functions as it is in the U.S.

  – The department appears very close-knit; indeed, you have rarely observed so many desks crowded into one office area. To your surprise, the section chief's desk is located in the same office space.

  – Salespeople are not appraised according to individual output; there is no quota system in place, only a semi-formal tracking of hours worked.

  – The salesforce, by and large, seems uncomfortable focusing on product benefits and going for the close when meeting with prospects.

  Your findings give you cause for anxiety. Your recommendations mostly centered around the need for sales training and tighter performance tracking (for individuals, not just the team as a whole). You also brought up – not as a recommendation but as an idea to think about – the possibility of bringing in an expatriate sales manager, to serve as a helpful resource.

  Ishihara-san obliquely indicated that he did not think that additional performance control mechanisms would be beneficial to the department. He also stated that "it would be very difficult to get the salespeople all together for a day or two for a training class." He gave no comment regarding your suggestion as to an expatriate manager. On the whole, you found his feedback exasperating and wondered why, if he was going to shoot your ideas down, he would not at least give you the courtesy of explaining why he thought you were wrong.

- In regard to control and finance, you have been pleased. From what you can see, the General Manager is hands-on with even small details of financial control. Perhaps in the future there might be the need to help those in accounting prepare financial statements and budget forecasts that are a little more in line with Western accounting procedures, but for now, you are basically satisfied. You did mention to Suzuki-san that in the future more detail might need to be reported as to entertainment expenses, gifts and contributions. This was met, as far as you can tell, with an attitude of relative acceptance. After all, you certainly learned in the first phase of negotiations that business conducted in Japan demands far more attention to relationships – and thus necessitates additional spending.

  One thing that was a little unsettling was the section chief's response to an item of information you gave him. You know that, in the next few months, there will be a fairly significant re-structuring of your division. You aren't sure exactly what this will entail and what impact, if any, it will have upon the joint venture company. However, as a sign of trust and to prepare Suzuki-san for any potential changes in reporting requirements, you thought you would tell him the news.

JAPANESE SCENARIO (Cont'd)

You were sorry you did; his reaction did not convey to you that he was glad you had "let him in" on the upcoming re-structuring. He did not ask the follow-up questions one would expect; there was, in fact, no discussion at all. After a longish pause, he then proceeded to ask you questions on a completely different topic, regarding some minor points of a specific request you'd made to him earlier.

- In regard to personnel, your primary issue was that of reducing the number of workers in manufacturing, should the production process be streamlined.

  A minor issue that puzzled you, though, involved a conversation you had with a bright young manager reporting to Atarashi-san. This manager had received his M.B.A. in the U.S. at a prestigious university and, in your opinion, had some ideas that were quite good in regard to recruiting. However, when you asked him what the section chief thought of these ideas, he became rather silent. Guessing that – for whatever reason – this promising manager was not able to discuss new ideas with his section chief, you suggested that he approach the General Manager, who you knew would appreciate his suggestions.

  This manager retreated from the conversation, giving a few vague replies. You sat for a minute in the office in which you had been speaking and wondered when you would ever understand the Japanese.

BEING PREPARED

Let's imagine an individual called Mr. U.S. has created his own cultural profile and also one for Japan. He can now compare the profiles and identify critical differences for which he should prepare.

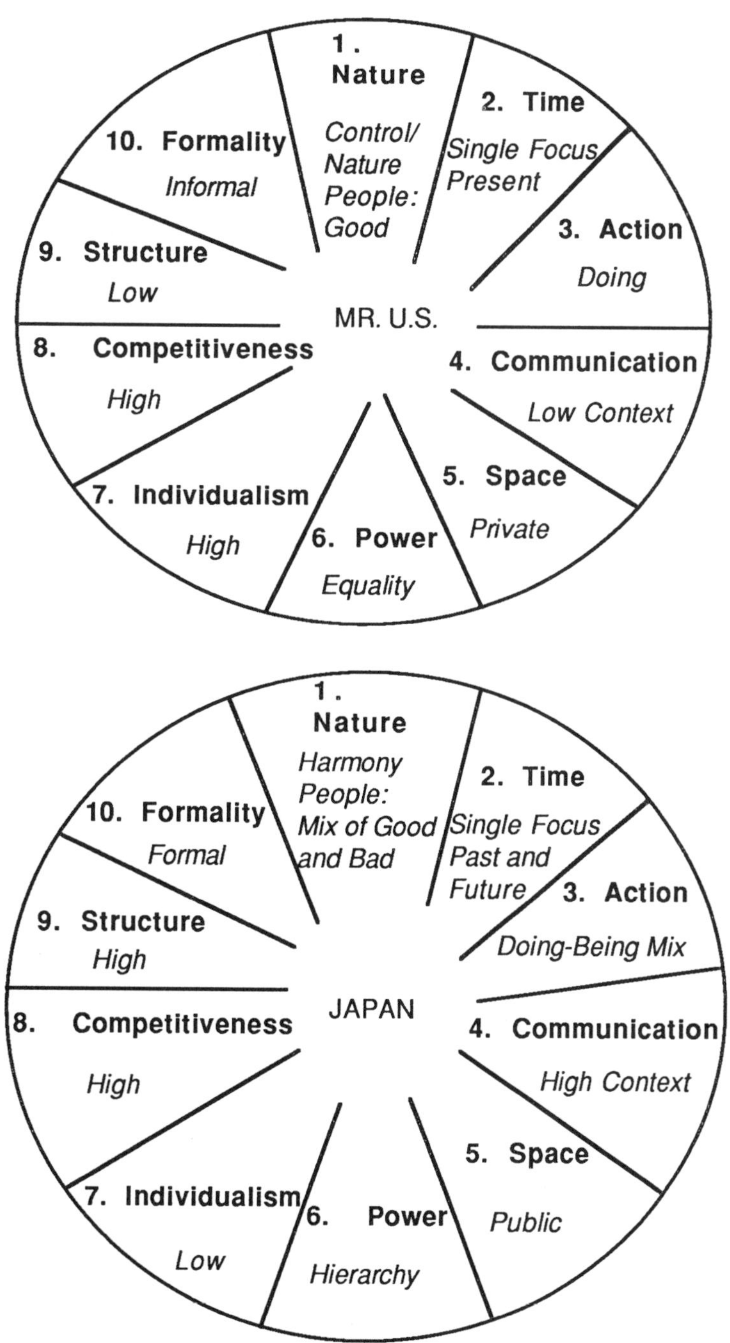

Review Question 19:

How does your own cultural profile compare with the Japanese profile drawn above? What critical differences would you prepare for?

CROSS-CULTURAL AWARENESS: DEVELOPMENT PRIORITIES

After reviewing the material in **Module 2: Cross-Cultural Awareness**, describe what you consider to be your top three personal development priorities and those of your organization. For your personal development priorities, be as specific as you can be, e.g., description, action steps and dates.

Development Priority #1	
Personal:	Organization:

Development Priority #2	
Personal:	Organization:

Development Priority #3	
Personal:	Organization:

MODULE 3: CROSS-CULTURAL COMMUNICATION

Overview

Primary Objective: Identify and overcome intercultural communication barriers in order to achieve greater effectiveness and synergy.

Units:

A: The Communication Process

B. Doing Things Differently: Business and Social Etiquette

C: Handling Cross-Cultural Differences

Communication takes place when you share the same meaning with someone else. This can be difficult with someone from your own culture. The difficulties are often multiplied many times over when you're trying to communicate with someone from another culture. You cannot assume that what is "common sense" to you is "common sense" to someone else. Appropriate colors to wear can be important if you are not to offend your host; the same gesture of the hand can mean O.K. in one culture and be obscene in another; inquiring about female members of a family may be considered very impolite in some cultures and friendly in others. While understanding the cross-cultural communication process is very helpful, you also need to be prepared to handle cross-cultural differences and adapt your negotiation style to fit the situation. We will all make mistakes when doing business internationally; the critical factors are to minimize the number of mistakes we make, learn from those we do make, and move on more effectively.

UNIT A: THE COMMUNICATION PROCESS

Objectives

After completing this unit, you will be able to:

 Recognize cultural synergy as a key communication objective.

 Identify the basic elements of the communication process.

 Identify major barriers to cross-cultural communication.

 Apply cross-cultural communication guidelines.

CULTURAL SYNERGY: A KEY COMMUNICATION OBJECTIVE

Cultural diversity can be a strength. The cultural synergy viewpoint assumes that while we may share certain similarities, we have fundamental differences that can add value. There are many ways of achieving the same results, and by sharing our differences we can create an approach that is greater than the sum of our individual contributions. This requires us to manage diversity, rather than try to ignore or minimize its effects.

Synergistic companies integrate the best of the cultures represented in their organizations. They view diversity not as an obstacle to be overcome but as a **resource** for adding value and creating advantage.

Maximizing cultural synergy should be a primary objective in any of your cross-cultural interactions.

WHY COMMUNICATE?

As an international manager, you will be performing the vast majority of tasks that you've always done: Planning, Organizing, Leading, Controlling, Staffing, etc. All of them involve communication of one sort or another. Now you will also have the added dimension of culture. Culture is both a **challenge** and an **opportunity**.

The challenge is to overcome the significant barriers to effective cross-cultural communication and convey meaning in a clear, precise and persuasive manner to facilitate productivity.

The opportunity is to build synergistic cross-cultural relationships that serve as the foundation for a global competitive advantage.

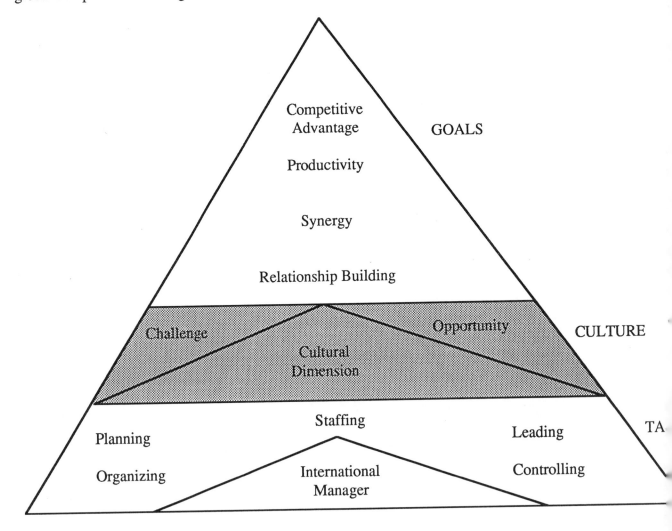

COMMUNICATION PROCESS

When communication is successful, the sender and receiver share the same meaning. Whatever the receiver perceives and interprets is part of the message; this may include words (verbal) and facial expressions, eye contact, gestures, and tone of voice (non-verbal).

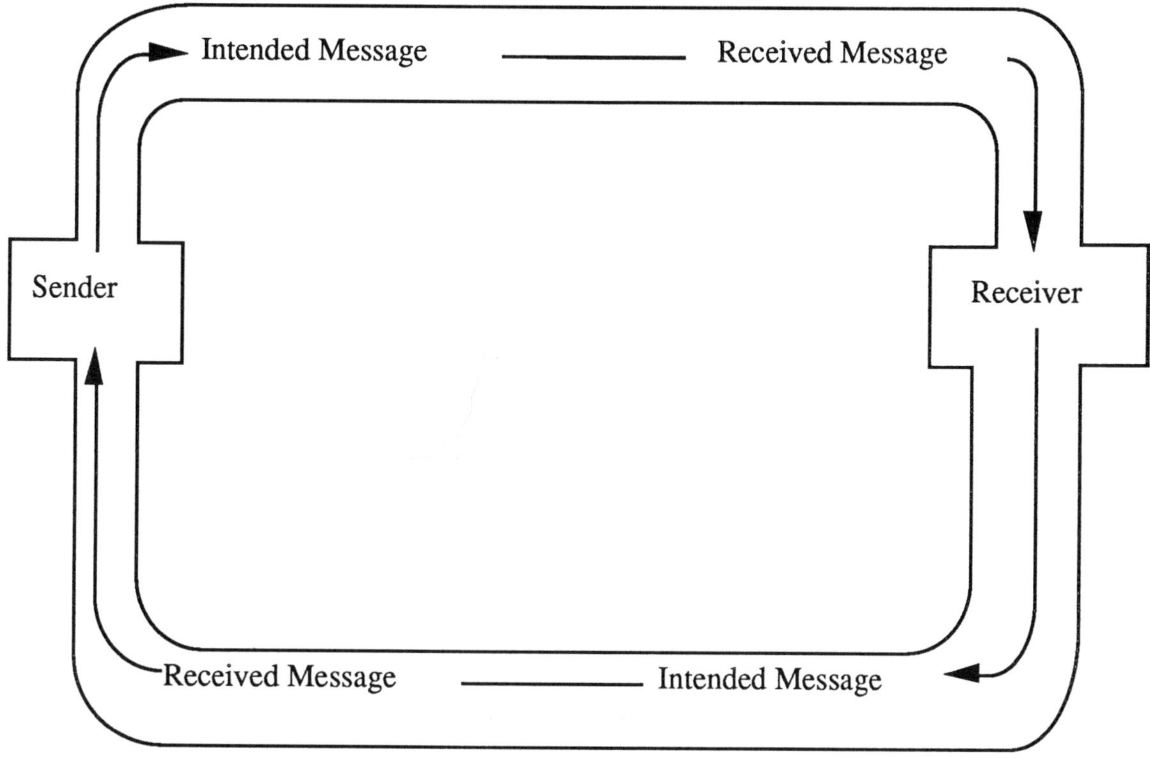

Perception is the key to communication and perception is largely determined by culture. Culture acts as a **filter** and focuses our attention on what is considered to be significant and meaningful.

COMMUNICATION BARRIERS

Differences in culture mean differences in perception. The potential for miscommunication is greatly increased when the sender and receiver do not share cultural perceptions.

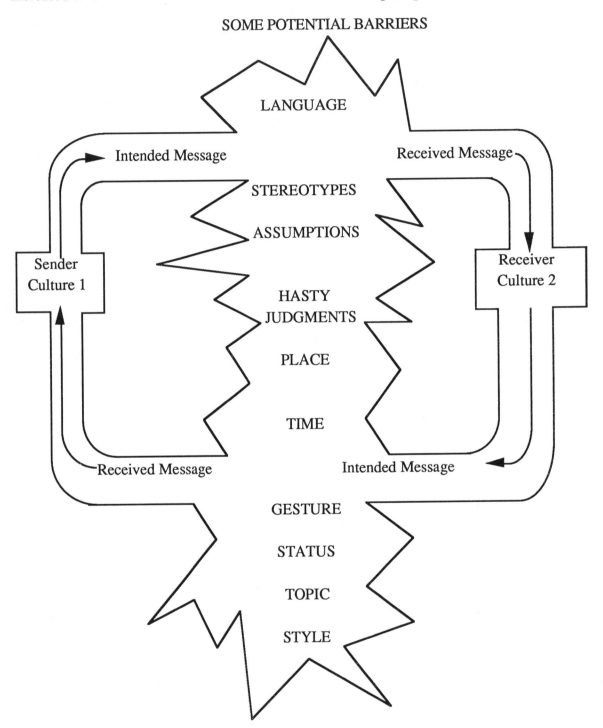

The greater the differences between Culture 1 and Culture 2, the greater the possibility for misunderstanding.

BARRIERS EXPLAINED

Barrier	Explanation
Language	The greatest barrier of all. All of the people may speak English, but there can still be misunderstandings. For example, when an English woman at a meeting in America says, "and I'd like to *table* another item," the Americans think she wants to postpone talking about that issue or put it aside altogether. Instead, she wants to bring it to their attention. Stay simple and slow paced. Avoid jargon, slang, unusual idioms, colloquialisms. Check for understanding. Learn at least the basics of the other language.
Stereotypes	Stereotypes can blind us to realities. They are crude generalizations based on prejudices rather than reliable data. However, if you are aware of the stereotype of the group you are dealing with, it's possible that it may help you in the beginning of an interaction. If you don't use it to start evaluating the other group, but simply to orient yourself to their differences, it may help you. If you get stuck in the stereotype and don't pay attention to the individuals you're working with, you could end up in trouble. Be alert to the fact that the other side may be working with stereotypes of you – "The Brash American," "The English Snob," "The Arrogant Frenchman." If you feel that a stereotype is being used against you, display behavior in contradiction to the expectations.
Assumptions	We all make assumptions. Sometimes they're correct and sometimes they're not. Assume you're a salesperson. A potential client says, "I'll give you a call soon and let you know if I'm going to buy." What do you assume by 'soon'? Americans might assume within 2 or 3 days. Hispanics, within 1 to 3 months. The Chinese may assume within the next year.

BARRIERS EXPLAINED (Cont'd)

Barrier	Explanation
Hasty Judgments	Hasty judgments are the result of immediately reacting to the given message through a cultural "filter," without stopping to check for a correct interpretation. An example: an American accountant was sent to Japan to teach to members of an affiliate company the fundamentals of U.S. financial practices. The American was surprised and delighted by the depth of knowledge among his Japanese counterparts. Out of curiosity, he said, "How did you get such good training in our methods?" The Japanese reacted defensively, assuming that the American was attacking their authority and competence. They didn't check their understanding of what the American was saying.
Time and Place	We all know the old saying, "There's a time and a place for every-thing." The holiest time in the Moslem year is Ramadan, which lasts for 30 days. To be considerate, and avoid upsetting your hosts, don't eat, drink or smoke in front of people during the daylight hours.
Gesture	The American gesture of O.K. – touching the index finger to the thumb and making a circle – is an obscene insult to the Greeks, the Brazilians, and the Turks. It could bring conversation to a close very quickly. The Japanese point with their middle finger, which is close to an obscene gesture for Americans. To a Saudi, showing the soles of your feet is a definite insult, and you would never pass a piece of paper with your left hand – that hand is reserved for personal cleanliness.
Status	Observing status differences in most cultures in the world is quite important. Deference to rank and respect for hierarchical levels is important in many Latin American, Asian, and European cultures. For example, if you want to kill communication in Mexico, invite all levels of employees and management to a staff meeting. The man-agers will be insulted. If you want to show disrespect to an East Asian senior negotiator, do not show any particular deference to him relative to the other members of the negotiating team.

BARRIERS EXPLAINED (Cont'd)

Barrier	Explanation
Topic	It is important to know in advance what conversational topics are and are not appropriate. For example, the British are always eager to talk about the weather. Don't make fun of the Royal Family, the British affection for animals, or the "work ethic." Politics and World War II can be sensitive subjects in Germany. When in France, avoid talking about business during meals, unless your host gives a signal that it is O.K.
Style	In general, avoid conversation about money and the cost of items, age, sex, politics, and comparisons with your own culture. The direct style of American communication is not to everyone's taste. The "get to the point," "let's not waste any time" efficiency-driven mode of communication is insulting or considered pushy in many cultures. The American style of *inductive* thinking and communicating, (i.e., beginning at the end, the conclusion) is also not everyone else's pattern of choice. For example, the French are trained *deductively*. They will start at the beginning and follow each logical step to the conclusion. Building the case takes time and frustrates Americans.

TAKING RESPONSIBILITY: ACTIVE LISTENING AND ACTIVE OBSERVING

It is difficult to avoid all the barriers to cross-cultural communication at all times. It helps if you **take responsibility** for the communication. Active listening and observing are key to taking responsibility.

Some cultures refer to the mind as the "Mad Monkey." It never rests; it jumps from one bit of information to another. Focusing its attention is hard work. It can "tune out," but it can also be "tuned in."

- **Passive listening and looking** = "tuning out," faking comprehension, pretending to pay attention. Hearing without listening. Looking without seeing.

  Passive listening and looking is a denial of responsibility for the communication.

- **Active listening and looking** = "tuning in," working at getting meaning, paying closer attention to details and nuances.

  Active listening and looking accept responsibility for the communication.

When making deals, or trying to increase productivity, you can't afford to deny responsibility for the communication.

Tips

Listening	Observing
• Concentrate, avoid distractions. • Listen for central ideas. • Ask questions. • Check yourself for cultural assumptions. • Try to interpret from the other's cultural perspective as well as from your own. • Restate and paraphrase to confirm and clarify. • Listen to content, not delivery. • Listen for silence. Don't rush to fill in the gaps. • Postpone evaluations.	• Try to learn the body language code of the culture. • Focus clearly on the behavior and the setting. • Don't project your own meanings onto the behavior. Keep an open mind. • Don't make too many assumptions from *one* gesture, movement or sign. Pay attention to *consistent* touching, postures, eye movement, facial expressions, body movements and personal space requirements.

CROSS-CULTURAL COMMUNICATION GUIDELINES

Keep the following cross-cultural communication tips in mind.

- Work at understanding your own cultural preferences – Nature, Time, Action, Space, etc.
- Work at understanding and integrating into your own behavior the preferences of the other culture including the fundamentals of their language.
- Recognize your own cultural filters, especially stereotypes. Consider how members of the other culture may be using stereotypes of you and what you can do to overcome those sterotypes.
- Don't assume the other culture is similar to your own until you have received confirmation. Then check again, and again. Beware of jokes. They may not communicate well.
- Speak at a comfortable pace for your foreign associates. Don't raise your voice. Use visuals and print to support what you say. Don't use colloquialisms, jargon or slang.
- Break information into small chunks and present one chunk at a time.
- Repeat what was said. Summarize. Confirm. Clarify.
- Don't pre-judge or rush into hasty evaluations. Respect differences. Listen, observe, and describe rather than evaluate.
- Develop empathy. See the situation from your own and the other culture's perspective.
- Don't settle for the surface meaning. Patiently search for what is *really* being communicated.
- Respect the appropriate level of formality in the other culture.
- Avoid taboos. Pay particular attention to your non-verbal behavior.
- Have realistic expectations. Seek help when you think you're running into trouble.
- Recover from mistakes gracefully. Don't become defensive, withdrawn, or hostile.
- Above all, work at making relationships not just deals.

COMMUNICATION BARRIERS AT WORK

Apply all that you have learned about cross-cultural communication in the unit and analyze the following critical incidents for:

- What barriers hindered communications and how they served to create cross-cultural conflict.
- What the protagonist in each incident could have done to prevent or resolve the conflict.

Suggested answers are given in Appendix D on pages D7-D8.

Study Question 6:
What communication barriers are at work in this incident and how could they be overcome?

Alan Richardson was assigned to head up the relatively new marketing department of his company's off-shore office in Mexico City. He was very excited about this career opportunity – and the chance to use his fluent Spanish. His overall responsibility was to increase marketing's visibility and role, and bring new personnel on as well. With increasing competition in Mexico, U.S headquarters communicated to Alan that he was to bring the department in line with those in other international offices.

Alan called his first meeting in his office on Friday afternoon with the men who had been handling prior marketing efforts and all support staff. After everyone arrived, he greeted them briefly and promptly began the meeting. The first item on his agenda was to ask for suggestions as to how they might increase sales by using promotional campaigns. After a short discussion, he then proposed that the two primary marketing researchers, Eduardo and Miguel, look into a marketing research system, thinking that whoever proved to be the better researcher would be promoted to manager. He concluded the meeting by thanking them for their time and saying that the group would meet again next week to share information.

The group sat silently until Alan said in the fluent Spanish that he had been speaking all day, "That's all for now, guys. Have a good weekend."

Next week at the follow-up meeting, he was surprised to find that no one in the group had anything to suggest or report on.

Your answer:

COMMUNICATION BARRIERS AT WORK

Study Question 7:
What communication barriers are at work in this incident and how could they be overcome?

Cynthia Greene, a manager with a multinational insurance company, was daily becoming more frustrated in her work regarding the company's business unit in the U.K. Her project team needed the advice and input of the unit's director to complete a very important project satisfactorily; however, the director never seemed to be available to Cynthia's British counterparts. Several times over the last few weeks, she had left messages and faxes for her co-workers expressing her need for critical input from Mr. Thomas, the director. Her co-workers had agreed with her that this would help move things along considerably; however, it seemed that no one would take the initiative to request Mr. Thomas's involvement in the project. Cynthia felt uncomfortable about approaching Mr. Thomas herself, assuming that such a request would be better received if it came directly from one of the British staff members who had been working with him for a while.

However, after several weeks of no action, Cynthia called Mr. Thomas herself with a request for his involvement. She presented him with a plan that required direct action from him in several areas, as well as information that was in his area of expertise. She was received politely and thanked for her thoughts and recommendations.

Another week passed, however, and Cynthia found herself feeling increasingly isolated from her counterparts. The small social interactions that used to characterize their telephone calls and correspondence became less frequent and a "coldness" seemed to pervade their communications.

Your answer:

UNIT B: DOING THINGS DIFFERENTLY: BUSINESS AND SOCIAL ETIQUETTE

Objectives

After completing this unit, you will be able to:

 Recognize differences in business and social etiquette.

 Apply cross-cultural etiquette guidelines.

WHAT CAN GO WRONG?

One of the key cultural variables presented in Module 2 is formality. Business and social etiquette are extremely important in establishing and maintaining rapport. Many mistakes will be forgiven. You are the foreigner and it's expected that you will be different. Continue to be aware, however, that slips in protocol and continual "bad manners" can damage your own and your company's reputation.

At this point, please become familiar with the reference materials in Appendix C: Business and Social Etiquette In Specific Countries.

On the next page you will find an International Business Quiz. Refer to the materials in Appendix C and answer each question.

Refer to the etiquette guidelines before you are about to travel to one of the countries listed.

INTERNATIONAL BUSINESS QUIZ

Suggested answers can be found in Appendix D on page D9.

1. When greeting a man in France, should you address him by his first name or last name?

2. Are flowers considered a good gift for a hostess in Germany?

3. What type of conversation is appropriate for a business dinner in France?

4. Is it polite to inquire about family in Saudi Arabia?

5. In Germany, if you are invited to a business dinner, should your spouse accompany you?

ETIQUETTE GUIDELINES

You cannot prepare for every possible *faux pas*. But you can and should keep the following guidelines in mind.

Guidelines	Description
Watch Your Manners	Be more polite and formal in a foreign culture than you would be in your own. It's a great temptation to drop the formalities when away from home. Resist the temptation. Don't lead with a first name or a casual phrase like 'Hi.' Stay formal until you are invited to use more familiar terms. Know when to shake hands and bow.
Communicate Respect	Take time to learn names and titles and their correct pronunciations. Learn some of the host country's language, but make sure your pronunciation is good; small differences can have dramatic results. Don't insult the host by simply talking louder if he or she doesn't appear to understand. Learn the culture's customs regarding the giving of gifts (also know your company's policy towards gift giving as well as any legal restrictions of your own or your host's country). Criticism in public may cause someone to lose face. Know when, where, and how to confront. The giving and receiving of business cards can also be an important ceremony, particularly in East Asia. Handle business cards with care, take the time to read the card after you are given it, use two hands for giving and receiving, and keep them in a special holder. Dress somewhat conservatively; better to be safe than sorry.
Show Patience	The use of time differs across cultures. Impatience may cause you and your host stress, destroy the relationship, and lose you business. Don't expect to be received on time wherever you go, even if you have a scheduled appointment.
Be Gracious	You are a representative of your culture and your company twenty-four hours a day. Accept and give appropriate hospitality. When entertaining, understand local customs in relation to alcohol and appropriate foods. For example, Muslims don't drink alcohol or eat pork; Hindus don't eat beef.
Prepare Well and Seek Confirmation	Learn about the foreign culture before making your visit. But don't assume too much. Pay particular attention to the unseen (backstage) aspects of culture and individual differences. Whenever you can, check your understanding.

UNIT C: HANDLING CROSS-CULTURAL DIFFERENCES

Objectives

After completing this unit, you will be able to:

 Identify cultural responses to conflict.

 Recognize the major sources of intercultural conflict.

 Recognize the positive and negative aspects of conflict.

 Identify possible modes for resolving conflict.

 Identify key aspects of cross-cultural negotiation.

CULTURAL RESPONSES TO CONFLICT

Cross-cultural relations, like other relations, involve conflict. Conflict happens; it is inevitable. As we said when discussing the Global Manager Paradigm, you need to see conflict as an opportunity for creating synergy and enhanced decision making.

Although you need to perceive conflict as normal, you also need to understand that different cultures respond to conflict differently .

Culture	Response
Japan	The Japanese view *'Wa'* – harmony – as a critical value. They will, therefore, communicate indirectly and avoid open conflict. Face-saving is paramount. Emotions should be hidden.
France	The French expect and even enjoy some degree of conflict. Their educational system encourages debate. Furthermore, the style of individualism found in France is such that individuation (or the surfacing of individual differences in conflict) is an integral part of communication – and even communicates respect.
Mexico	While accepting the inevitability of conflict, Mexicans deal with it indirectly and will avoid it if possible. Face saving to preserve honor and dignity is crucial. However, if the conflict must be dealt with, the approach is emotional and sometimes passionate.
USA	Conflict is natural; direct confrontation and even a "winner-take-all" viewpoint is typical. Both sides are expected to fight for what they want, and compromise is a typical solution. The approach is impersonal rather than emotional.

Conflict is neither "good" nor "bad" in itself. It can be positive and lead to learning or it can be negative and result in wasted energy and destroyed relationships.

SOURCES OF CONFLICT

Conflict can result at any time from the issues of how, what, when, where, and why. The disagreement may originate in substantive or emotional concerns. It may involve individuals or groups.

Take any one of the ten cultural variables we've outlined and you will find potential conflict.

Variable	Example
Nature	"What do you mean, you won't give me a five year plan?" *"It could be a sin if I did that."* "Well, God may be in charge of all things, but I still need a plan." *"I can't do that."*
Time	"I just want to meet this Quarter's sales objectives." *"But in the longer term we're going to lose customers if we can't maintain our customer service standard."* "We'll worry about that when the time comes."
Action	"But I'm offering you a substantial bonus if you get the project done in half the time." *"Money. Is that all you think about?"*
Communication	"So, do we have a deal?" *"It's difficult."* "Yes, but do we have a deal?" *"I'll try."* "What do you mean, you'll try?" *"It's difficult."*
Space	"This is the office you're giving me? A space in the middle of everyone else?" *"It is the most appropriate space for you."* "I don't care. I want an office with windows, and some privacy." *"That is not appropriate."*
Power	"But I told you to make the decision." *"But you're the boss."* "Yes. I'm the boss and I'm telling you to make the decision." *"But you're the boss."*
Individualism	"My cousin is coming in this afternoon. I'd like you to hire him for a job in administration." *"But, what can he do? Is he experienced?"* "What do you mean? He's my cousin!"

SOURCES OF CONFLICT (Cont'd)

Competitiveness	"If we do this we can double profits within six months." *"But at what cost! We'd lose two thirds of our staff working under that kind of pressure. It wouldn't be fair to them."*
Structure	"I want you to write detailed procedures for the new process." *"Well, it's pretty self-explanatory. You just..."* "I want detailed procedures."
Formality	"I would appreciate you knocking before you walk in my office." *"Hey, I'm sorry. The door was open."* "My door is always open. But that doesn't mean you can just walk in here whenever you feel like it."

We have talked a good deal about empathy and patience. But do you have limits? Absolutely!

You should be very clear in your own mind that you will not compromise your organization's core values or break the law.

Review Question 20:

Think of a conflict you've had with another person (ideally a person from another culture). What cultural preferences do you think were at odds with each other? How did you resolve the situation?

SWITCHING CONFLICT RESOLUTION STYLES

What do you do when faced with conflict? You may find yourself being one of the following types on a consistent basis. No one style is the *correct* one. You need to have the flexibility to adapt your style to the situation and the culture.

Style	Description
Commander	Uses formal power position to make decisions and resolve conflict. Cultures with pronounced hierarchies – such as the Phillipines, Panama, Malaysia, France, and the Latin American countries – expect managers to act with authority, to be decisive. There is often a clear demarcation between manager and subordinate, with the manager as expert and leader whose word is a command.
Problem Solver	Wants to draw on the expertise, values, and skills of the group to solve problems and create a win/win result. This can be difficult in highly individualistic cultures such as the United States where individuals compete against each other. Also, in collective societies where harmony is valued, individuals may feel intimidated by having to make contributions that set them apart from the others. Countries valuing structure may also have difficulty with this strategy.
Avoider	Tries to solve problem by denying its existence or withdrawing. In a culture which values direct communication, this can result in further conflict and stress. In societies where "saving face" is of great importance, however - Japan and other countries of the Far East, for example – this strategy may be the most appropriate, especially if the problem is a minor one.
Harmonizer	Wants to smooth over differences, supress disagreements and maintain a surface harmony. In cultures where individualism is valued, this can result in resentment and hostility. It would, however, be most appropriate for cultures like China that prize the group over the individual.
Negotiatior	Looks for compromise. Can be effective in all cultures. If the negotiator, however, makes a lot of early concessions, he or she may be perceived as weak and lose credibility. This would certainly be the case in Latin American countries or Russia.

Review Question 21:

Do you think one of the conflict resolution styles described above would have been more effective for dealing with the conflict you identified in Review Question 20?

CROSS-CULTURAL NEGOTIATION

As an international manager, you could spend between 50-60% of your time in some form of negotiating.

Cultures have different styles of negotiating and view the purposes of negotiation differently.

For example:

Japan	• Collaborative process - "mind meeting." • Several meetings before substantive issues are on the table. • Emphasis on harmony in relationships. Avoid open conflict. • Resolve conflict through harmonious cooperation coupled with assertiveness and persistence. • Avoid addressing issues directly and openly stating positions and counter positions. • Use of ambiguous language. • Goal is a just and proper deal and long-term harmonious relationship.
Germany	• Competitive process. • Negotiations planned and well organized. • Conflict seen as dysfunctional and a symptom of being unprepared; it wastes time that could be used for more useful discussion. • Direct in approach. • Discussion is precise and centered on facts.

KEY COMPONENTS IN NEGOTIATION: GETTING OUT OF THE BOX

Think about the main aspects of negotiation. They might look as follows:

REFRAMING

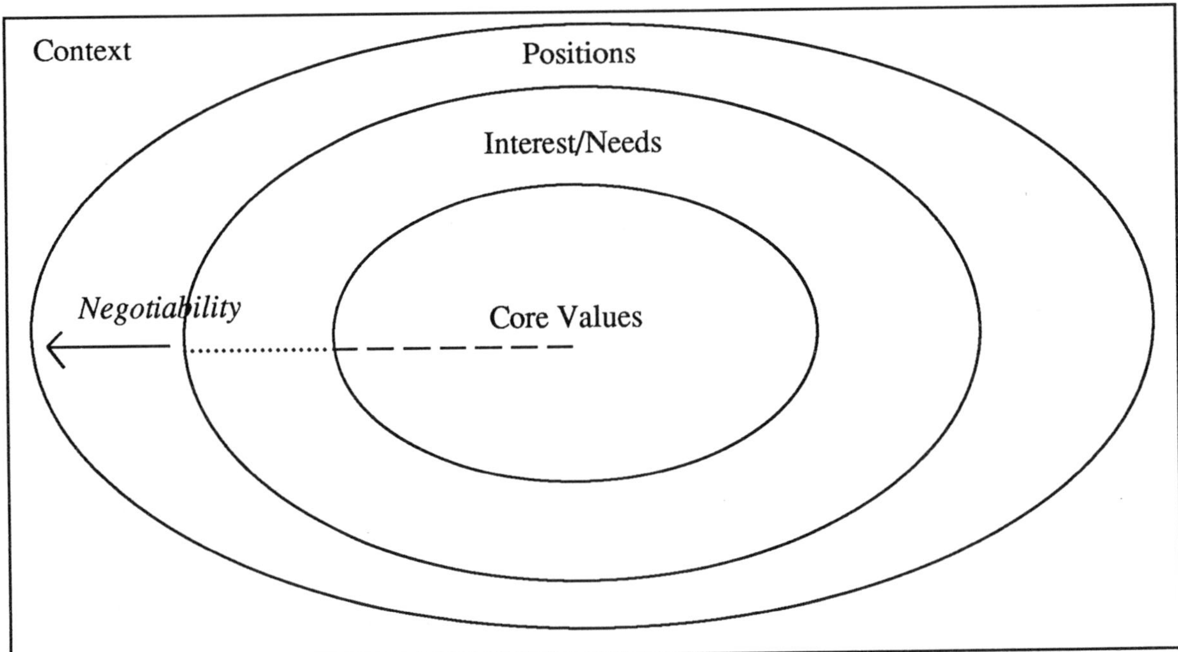

OPTIONALIZING

Legend

Negotiability
--- Very unlikely that core values can be negotiated
... Interests and needs, are somewhat negotiable
⟵ Likely that a position can be negotiated

All of the components in the box can trap you inside. Reframing and Optionalizing are deliberately put outside because that's where you may need to go to reach a satisfactory conclusion.

NEGOTIATION COMPONENTS

Core Values

Perhaps not articulated, but still playing a central role, are the cultural orientations of both sides. These are deeply held values and, though they may change slowly over time, they are, to a significant extent, not open to negotiation.

Interests/Needs

Refers to what both sides really want. They may be expressed in the actual stated positions; more often they are beneath the surface. The psychologist Abraham Maslow identified a hierarchy of basic needs from Physiological, to Safety/Security, to Social, to Esteem, and finally to Self-Actualization. Different cultures rearrange this hierarchy in a different order. For example, many Asian countries stress Social needs over Self-Actualization.

Positions

People tend to adopt one position on how their interests and needs can be met. They are stated as demands or preferences. Positions can lock you in the box. Focus on the underlying interests and needs and not on the stated position.

Context

This refers to the range of verbal and non-verbal behaviors being displayed, the physical setting of the negotiation, and the differences in key factors such as power, information, and time; these latter three factors play a very important role in shaping a negotiation.

Reframing

This is related to the idea of a paradigm shift. Can the problem be redefined? Is there a problem? What if we look at it upside down, back-to-front, inside out, sideways?

Optionalizing

The more options that can be identified, the more chances there are for a successful outcome.

NEGOTIATION PHASES AND GUIDELINES

Negotiation can be divided into six major phases:

Phase	Guidelines
Preparing	• Decide whether negotiation is appropriate. • Understand the other culture's core value preferences. • Establish clear objectives for yourself and understand the other's objectives. • Determine your overall strategy. • Set agenda and ground rules.
Relating	• Separate the people from the problem. Build relationships. • Allow everyone to feel at ease. • Identify the limits of authority and map relationships of attendees. • Find style and pace that are comfortable to both sides. • Maintain self control. • Work at developing respect and trust. • Don't rush at "getting down to business, " unless appropriate.
Informing	• Avoid presenting a position (the one solution or acceptable outcome). • Focus on interests based on needs. • Listen and observe as well as talk. • Tolerate ambiguity while seeking clarification. • Demonstrate confidence, not arrogance.
Persuading	• Spend a large amount of time exploring common ground, not just differences. • Look for and create options that offer mutual benefits. • Focus on the long term as well as the short term. • Position proposals to highlight benefits to the other side. • Set a range on your negotiable limits rather than a fixed point.
Choosing	• Don't resort to dirty tricks. Build the relationship. • Avoid making early concessions, unless appropriate. Know which concessions you would be willing to make. • Be objective, not emotional. Don't give in to pressure.
Agreeing	• It is better to walk away from a deal that gives you no benefits than merely make a deal. • Appreciate that there may not be a definite conclusion to a single meeting. • Appreciate that it is one thing to get an agreement and another to get the agreement implemented.

NEGOTIATION: LOST IN TAIWAN

Review the following incident and answer the questions on page 3-29.

Ellen Stoddard-Jones, 35, is a sales representative with a multinational data systems company headquartered in New York. While most of the firm's international business was conducted in Europe and Japan, China was a growing market for its products.

Ellen, a capable and ambitious graduate with a dual M.B.A./Ph.D. from a prestigious European university, had recently been transferred to her firm's International Division, where she was responsible for the Far East market. For the third time in two years, Ellen was scheduled to meet with representatives of a very large Taiwanese distributor whose product lines fit those of her company.

Her first trip to Taiwan had been basically positive but somewhat unsettling. Very little business had been discussed. To a certain extent, though, she'd expected that. She had been told by several more internationally-experienced co-workers that the Taiwanese would undoubtedly spend most of the time establishing a relationship, initiating culture-related trips during her stay, and showing respect for her and her company by providing entertainment. This had indeed been the case. Although she had enjoyed seeing places like the National Palace Museum in Taipei, she still had found this slow approach to achieving business goals frustrating. Ellen made sure that, upon her return to the U.S., she followed up with extensive communications regarding developing a contract.

Her second trip had fallen more in line with her expectations as to what a business trip should be, probably because she tried to take a more forceful lead in the negotiations. She had almost a full week of meetings with her primary contact, Chen Wu-Ping, and his colleagues. The Taiwanese team had seemed enthusiastic throughout the week about how well her company and theirs "fit." There were many comments from Chen Wu-Ping in particular about how he "looked forward to a long-lasting business relationship" and was "honored" to have Ellen come a second time to Taipei to continue the negotiations. Furthermore, the Taiwanese clearly recognized the superiority of her firm's product lines; they praised the reputation of her company and the quality of its products at some length. She was a little surprised when, in speaking about their own firm's qualifications, the Taiwanese were very modest. She knew that the distributor was among the best in the region. Ellen figured this could only work to her advantage; they obviously regarded this opportunity as a very beneficial deal.

By the end of the week, she was convinced that she had a firm agreement for a large contract. True, she had not left with a signed contract (although she had pressed to create one). But she understood that decisions in Taiwan probably take longer than in the U.S. and she was convinced of the ultimate success of her approach. Chen Wu-Ping had said that "Something will happen soon." She told her management that she expected a signed contract by the end of the quarter.

The goal for the third trip was to return with a signed contract, yet the introductory meetings during the first two days perplexed Ellen. She had thought that the contract was virtually sewn up, but the Taiwanese were not treating it as such. They were re-negotiating major points of the proposal, speaking of needing "more time" to discuss the contract, bringing up far-reaching implications of the contract that

NEGOTIATION: LOST IN TAIWAN (Cont'd)

were no concern of hers (such as potential effects on their relationships with other suppliers) and, in general, evading finalizing the agreement. There was also some confusion as to who exactly had the authority to make the decision to sign the contract. She had previously thought that Chen Wu-Ping was the decision maker; however, this did not seem to be the case now. He and his colleagues (all much older than she) did not seem to have an acknowledged leader.

Today's meeting was her chance to turn the situation around and find out conclusively whether or not Chen Wu-Ping and his colleagues would follow through on the agreement. Moving quickly through the small-talk, Ellen clearly elaborated the benefits and competitive advantages of her products over the competition, telling the Taiwanese distributors how this would help them get ahead. They asked many detailed questions about her products, which was surprising, since she had provided them long ago with substantial documentation outlining the specifications of the given product lines. She definitely felt the deal was slipping away and she was becoming increasingly anxious.

As the meeting progressed, the Taiwanese kept averting eye contact, even when she asked them direct questions. She pointed out that the deal was very competitively priced, but her words were followed by uncomfortable silence. Keying in on all the benefits they would receive by signing the contract, she proceeded to argue that her firm's products would revolutionize their somewhat-outdated methods, bring them praise from their management and colleagues for the gains in efficiency achieved, and save other companies millions of dollars. Also, many renowned companies throughout Europe were using these state-of-the-art products.

At the end of the meeting, the Taiwanese said that they would study her proposal further, but she felt that a company like hers shouldn't get this kind of treatment. Clearly, she was offering them the best products available. If they did not recognize all the advantages that Taiwanese companies would reap in terms of time and money savings, that was their fault.

A few weeks after Ellen returned to New York, she received word that the Taiwanese distributors had decided to forego signing the contract.

NEGOTIATION: LOST IN TAIWAN (Cont'd)

In analyzing the situation that you have just read about, consider the following questions. Suggested answers are given in Appendix D on pages D10-D13.

Study Question 8:

What do you think were the primary core values of both parties?

Your answer:

Study Question 9:

What were some of the underlying interests and needs of both parties?

Your answer:

Study Question 10:

What factors in the negotiation context helped or hindered the negotiations?

Your answer:

Study Question 11:

What could Ellen have done differently to move the negotiations along more successfully?

Your answer:

CROSS-CULTURAL COMMUNICATION: DEVELOPMENT PRIORITIES

After reviewing the material in **Module 3: Cross-Cultural Communication**, describe what you consider to be your top three personal development priorities and those of your organization. For your personal development priorities, be as specific as you can be, e.g., description, action steps and dates.

Development Priority #1	
Personal:	Organization:

Development Priority #2	
Personal:	Organization:

Development Priority #3	
Personal:	Organization:

MODULE 4: WORKING ACROSS CULTURES

Overview

Primary Objective: Adapt business skills to working in different cultural settings.

Units:

A: Culture and Management

B: Adapting Business Skills

C: Marketing and Sales

D: The International Manager: Success Factors

At the end of Module 2, you started work on the first two steps of developing cross-cultural awareness: 1. Self-Awareness and 2. Cross-Cultural Understanding. You are now ready for Step 3: Adapting Business Skills.

You may be sent to work overseas on a lengthy assignment. You may lead a project team that has members from a number of foreign subsidiaries. You may make a relatively short trip to another country to troubleshoot a problem. In all such cases, you need to prepare yourself to cope with diversity. You are accustomed to performing your management functions within your own culture. You and your employees share similar expectations and values. Within a foreign culture, how will you plan, organize, staff, lead, and control? What adjustments will you need to make? How will you market and sell across different cultural terrain? Learning how to learn is critical for the international manager: continuous learning from people, places, books, newspapers and other resources is a must.

UNIT A: CULTURE AND MANAGEMENT

Objectives

After completing this unit, you will be able to:

 Recognize the importance of cultural adaptation to management effectiveness.

 Identify the impact of cultural preferences on five management skill areas: Planning, Organizing, Staffing, Leading, and Controlling.

ARE WE GETTING CLOSER?

We talk of a "global village" connected by instant communications and fast transportation. We see global businesses and other organizations making an impact across the continents.

Do these factors mean that we are all growing closer together and sharing similar cultural values?

No.

- Global companies find that they must work with rather than against unique local cultures. Cultures and people resist change imposed from the outside; it can make them more determined to be different. Japan, for example, has adopted some western characteristics but has remained a cultural island.
- It is futile to introduce forms of management to people culturally unable to accept them. It leads to confusion and resentment. Rather, it is essential to adapt management style to cultural context.

Don't forget: Differences can add value. Synergy and creativity are built on the interaction of differences, not similarity or imposed conformity.

MANAGEMENT SKILL AREAS: OVERVIEW

Management involves the coordination of available human and non-human resources to achieve organizational objectives.

Many managerial activities are performed across all societies, although cultural orientations shape the activities to fit the environment.

In this program, we focus on five important management skill areas and the activities typical of each area. Be aware that the descriptions below have an American bias.

Planning: Establishing goals and objectives and determining the actions needed to achieve them.

- Determining planning methodology
- Defining goals and objectives
- Quantifying goals and objectives
- Determining current strengths and weaknesses
- Forecasting future trends in relation to goals and objectives
- Determining type and amount of information needed
- Choosing among alternative courses of action
- Building flexibility into the plan
- Implementing the plan
- Evaluating results
- Taking corrective action

Organizing: Dividing and coordinating work and resources to achieve maximum productivity

- Differentiating work tasks
- Producing job descriptions
- Determining formal role relationships
- Assigning tasks to appropriate people
- Allocating resources to achieve tasks
- Coordinating work through appropriate levels of supervision and control
- Establishing clear lines of communication

Staffing: Hiring appropriate people to fill jobs and helping those people to fulfill their potential

- Selecting recruitment methods
- Establishing selection/promotion criteria
- Determining performance appraisal criteria/ methods
- Orienting people to organization and jobs
- Identifying and meeting training needs
- Establishing compensation criteria/methods
- Determining dismissal criteria/procedures

Leading: Directing people toward fulfilling organization goals and objectives

- Determining appropriate leadership style
- Defining a vision and mission
- Inspiring commitment
- Directing and coordinating efforts
- Establishing decision-making procedures
- Delegating authority
- Resolving conflict and negotiating
- Solving problems
- Establishing employee development philosophy

Controlling: Monitoring performance and taking action to prevent or solve problems

- Identifying areas for control
- Identifying control techniques
- Establishing performance objectives and standards
- Designing and implementing feedback systems
- Comparing performance with objectives and standards
- Taking corrective action
- Integrating control criteria into plans

CULTURAL IMPACT SHEET: PLANNING

Variable	Potential Impact
Nature	Cultures that emphasize **control** over nature believe that the purpose of planning is to control the environment in order to achieve goals. Decision making in planning is goal and task oriented. Contracts and detailed action plans are considered the primary means of plan implementation. Change is viewed as positive and justified in terms of economic pay-offs. Risk forecasting is routine and is based upon analysis of forces to be overcome. Cultures that emphasize **harmony** with nature believe that plans should set goals but have flexibility built in to allow for environmental changes. Decision making addresses the contexts that need to be in harmony with the plan for it to be achieved (i.e., traditions, consensus with the involved parties, etc.). Trust between the parties is considered the surest means of plan implementation, although management techniques are utilized. Change is viewed as positive as long as it is not at variance with given contexts. Risk forecasting is a part of planning but it is understood that not all risks can be predicted. Cultures that emphasize **subjugation** to nature believe that it is presumptuous to claim control over the environment in planning. Decision making in planning is often ad hoc, intuitive and influenced by personal relationships. Close relationships (especially those with friends or family members), not management systems, are the key to plan implementation. Change is viewed as threatening and can be justified only to the degree that precedent can be found for the new action. Risk forecasting is not done, since outcomes of plans are seen as dependent upon complex social, political and religious forces.
Time	Cultures that are characterized by: • **Single focus** orientation to time are task and schedule focused in planning. • **Multi-focus** orientation to time are more focused on relationship building in planning. Cultures that are oriented to: • The **past** emphasize the continuance of traditions in planning and build in long time frames if the plan is for a change process. • The **present** emphasize short-term plans and aim at achieving quick results. • The **future** emphasize longer-term plans and long-term results.
Action	**"Doing"** cultures tend to plan by developing measurable, time-framed action steps. Emphasis is on the tasks to be achieved. **"Being"** cultures tend to plan by focusing more on the vision to be attained, i.e., the social, economic and philosophical gains to be achieved.

CULTURAL IMPACT SHEET: PLANNING (Cont'd)

Variable	Potential Impact
Communication	**Low context** cultures develop plans that are explicit, detailed, quantifiable, information-based and broken down into specific, individual accountabilities. **High context** cultures develop plans that are more implicit, less detailed in terms of instructions, relationship-based and group-oriented.
Space	**Private space** cultures tend toward more individualistic, task-based or systematic forms of planning. **Public space** cultures tend toward more group-oriented, relationship-based or authoritative forms of planning.
Power	Cultures that value **equality** display more participative planning in which managers consult with subordinates in the decision making. Employees may implement the plan in the way they believe is the most appropriate. There tends to be an emphasis on systems and strategic thinking. Cultures that value **hierarchy** display more autocratic or paternalistic planning, in which managers make decisions without consulting with subordinates. Employees implement the plan in the way the manager wants it performed. There tends to be an emphasis on personal planning (rather than systems) and "political" thinking (as relationships/connections may be the means for plan implementation).
Individualism	Cultures that value **collectivism** place greater value on group decisions than individual ones; expect that managers will gather the views of employees rather than have individual employees take the initiative; develop plans within the shared values used for measuring and justifying activities in the organization; and are more relationship-oriented in regard to plan formulation and implementation. Cultures with high **individualism** values place greater value on individual decisions than group ones; expect that all those involved in planning will take the initiative to present their views; develop plans according to inpersonal quantifiable calculations that can be used to measure performance; and are more task-oriented in regard to planning.
Competitiveness	Cultures that place a value on **cooperativeness** show a stronger belief in group decisions and define criteria for success more in terms of a service ideal. There is emphasis on maintaining relationships and quality of organizational life in plan implementation. Cultures that place a high value on **competitiveness** show a stronger belief in more independent decisions and define criteria for success more in terms of profits alone. There is an emphasis on speed and task performance in plan implementation.

CULTURAL IMPACT SHEET: PLANNING (Cont'd)

Variable	Potential Impact
Structure	**Low structure** value cultures practice strategic planning activities, which focus on broad goals; tend to leave planning to generalists and managers; have less need for clear role and responsibility definitions; show a preference for broad guidelines rather than specific methodologies; allow conflict and dissent in planning; display greater tolerance for uncertainty and less emotional resistance to change; and exhibit greater willingness to take risks. **High structure** value cultures have a need for more detail in planning with quantifiable goals and objectives; tend to leave planning to specialists; need clear role and responsibility definitions; show a preference for precise instructions and rules; prize harmony and consensus in planning; display stress in the face of uncertainty and emotional resistance to change; and exhibit less willingness to take risks.
Formality	**Informal** cultures do not display much concern for proper business and social etiquette when forming new business relationships in the planning stage. Goals, tasks, direct communication and a casual approach are valued. **Formal** cultures stress adherence to protocol throughout planning, particularly when establishing a new business relationship. Attention to hierarchy, rules, rituals and cultural traditions are valued, in addition to goals and tasks.

CULTURAL IMPACT SHEET: ORGANIZING

<table>
<tr><th>Variable</th><th>Potential Impact</th></tr>
<tr><td>Nature</td><td>Cultures that emphasize control over nature believe that the future can be planned for and achieved. Thus, organization is explicit, time-framed and action-oriented. Work packages are clear, as are lines of communication for monitoring and control.

Cultures that emphasize harmony with nature approach organization from a more cross-functional, holistic viewpoint. Decision makers consult all those who can contribute information to, give feedback on, or are involved with the areas being organized. Maintaining harmonious relationships between all the parties involved is a key value.

Cultures that emphasize subjugation to nature believe that the future is largely subject to forces beyond human action. Organizing is not guided so much by management methods (which assume that work can be planned for) as by the personal direction of those in power. Leadership style is autocratic, and subordinates are not included in organizing decisions.</td></tr>
<tr><td>Time</td><td>Cultures that are characterized by:
• Single focus orientation to time have a structured, linear, task-focused approach to organizing. Adherence to schedules is considered very important. Step-by-step performance of tasks is the model for organization.
• Multi-focus orientation to time have a more unstructured, holistic, people-focused approach to organizing. Schedules are not taken so seriously and may be changed should other priorities arise. Accomplishment of tasks in the context of shifting demands and building/maintaining relationships is the goal of organization.

Cultures that are oriented to:
• The past make organizational decisions within the context of the customs and traditions of the society. Past goals and precedents also guide the process of organizing.
• The present divide and coordinate work and resources based on present demands.
• The future divide and coordinate work and resources to meet longer-range goals and projections of the future.</td></tr>
<tr><td>Action</td><td>"Doing" cultures organize by developing action-oriented, project management documentation, with task responsibilities, schedules, monitoring and control mechanisms, reporting relationships and resource information clearly spelled out.

"Being" cultures organize more on the assumption that implementation is not so much dependent on action steps and documentation as on common vision, personal trust or shared sense of well being.</td></tr>
<tr><td>Communication</td><td>Low context cultures organize explicitly. Job descriptions, authority relationships, monitoring/control procedures, task-responsibility guidelines, etc., are detailed and understood through verbal or written instructions. Good relationships between the parties involved are generally not critical for task accomplishment.

High context cultures organize implicitly. Job descriptions, etc., are broader-based and understood contextually. Good relationships between the parties involved are important for task accomplishment.</td></tr>
</table>

CULTURAL IMPACT SHEET: ORGANIZING (Cont'd)

Variable	Potential Impact
Space	In general, **private space** cultures tend toward more task-centered organizational approaches and structured communications. **Public space** cultures tend toward more relationship-centered organizational approaches and less structured communications.
Power	Cultures that value **equality** decentralize authority and responsibility to the lowest possible level. Organizational structure encourages individual autonomy and responsibility. Employees do not like being closely supervised and feel comfortable with a participative supervisor. In boss-subordinate communications, employees aren't afraid to disagree with their managers. Cultures that value **hierarchy** centralize authority and responsibility. Organizational structure is tightly controlled. Employees like being closely supervised and feel comfortable with a directive/persuasive supervisor. Employees will not disagree with their managers.
Individualism	Cultures **high in collectivism** give little recognition to the individual except in the context of the group to which he/she belongs. Organizational structures emphasize the group; the team is assigned tasks and resources, and evaluated as a whole. Individual accountability is diffused into group identification; individually-prescribed responsibilities or job descriptions are avoided. Conformity to group/company standards and regulations is expected; managers aspire to conformity and security. Cultures high in **individualism** provide opportunity for individual recognition, accountability, and achievement. Organizational structures emphasize the individual; task assignments, resource allocation and performance appraisals are done on an individual basis. There is individual responsibility for results as well as clearly-defined job descriptions. Self-reliance and initiative are expected; managers aspire to leadership.
Competitiveness	Cultures that value **cooperation** structure work to permit group integration and satisfy such motivational factors as security, positive working environment and schedules that allow for a full personal/family life. Managers have more of a facilitative role. Cultures with high **competitiveness** values structure work to permit individual achievement and satisfy such motivational factors as high earnings, recognition, advancement and challenge. Managers have more of a leadership role.
Structure	Cultures with **low structure** values organize more on the basis of a pragmatic, situational decision making process. Job and task descriptions can be broadly-interpreted, and allow room for the employee to make his or her own decisions. Formal relationships may be less defined; hierarchical structures may be by-passed for practical reasons. Organizational forms allowing for conflict or competition are often preferred. Ambiguity causes less stress. Cultures with **high structure** values organize more on the basis of hierarchy and set rules and procedures. Job and task descriptions usually are composed of clear instructions, and the emphasis is on the employee to carry out these instructions. Formal relationships are defined; hierarchical structures should be respected. Organizational forms that allow for conflict and/or competition are not desirable. Ambiguity causes stress.

CULTURAL IMPACT SHEET: ORGANIZING (Cont'd)

Variable	Potential Impact
Formality	**Informal** cultures tend to be less hierarchy-conscious in organization and can challenge rules and procedures. Good business relationships are generally not seen as a pre-requisite to accomplishing work. Communication tends to be direct and candid. There is less deference given to those with higher status. **Formal** cultures tend to be more hierarchy-conscious in organization and accepting of rules and procedures. Good business relationships are considered important for accomplishing work. Communication tends to be more indirect and guided by protocol. There is greater deference given to those with higher status.

CULTURAL IMPACT SHEET: STAFFING

Variable	Potential Impact
Nature	Cultures that emphasize **control** over nature stress bottom-line performance and achievement with their employess. Staffing and promotion are based solely on merit. Employees are retained by the organization only as long as they have the skills needed to meet organizational objectives. Employment is not guaranteed beyond a limited contract. Cultures that emphasize **harmony** with nature try to guarantee long-term employment for their employees. Promotion is based on seniority as well as merit. The challenge is to staff and promote to achieve organizational goals; however, providing harmonious, stable tenure for employees is seen as pre-requisite to their effective performance. Cultures that emphasize **subjugation** to nature stress social and family background in staffing. Personal contacts rather than qualifications are key for advancement. The challenge is to select and advance personnel to ensure future security and trustworthiness. Once hired, employees will be retained; firing a person involves great loss of prestige.
Time	Cultures that are characterized by: • **Single focus** orientation to time are more focused on tasks than relationships in business and therefore generally have a shorter-term, untenured view of employment. • **Multi-focus** orientation to time are more focused on building long-term relationships in business and therefore generally have a longer-term, tenured view of employment. Cultures that are oriented to the: • **Past** are slower to adapt the criteria by which they select and train employees. Managers emphasize organizational loyalty and adherence to social/moral traditional customs. • **Present** select and train employees to meet current goals and environmental demands. Fast payoffs are often expected when hiring, training and developing employees. • **Future** select and train employees to meet longer-term business goals. Based on future benefits, companies will invest heavily in recruitment and employee development.
Action	In **"Doing"** cultures, career development is based upon achievement of agreed-upon goals and performance targets. Performance appraisal is based upon external, explicit standards of measurement. Motivation is by achievement, advancement, individual recognition and performance-tied bonuses. Ambition is expected and rewarded. Working relationships are more impersonal; it is not necessarily important to recognize a person's worth beyond his or her ability to fulfill organizational tasks. In **"Being"** cultures, career development is not only based upon performance but upon other standards, such as personal or social criteria, obligations, mentor relationships, loyalty to the company, character, values, etc. Performance appraisal is conducted more informally and sporadically. Persons are evaluated in such a way that the appraisal is not detrimental to the work environment and relationships. Overt ambition may be frowned upon. Personal recognition of a person's worth beyond his or her ability to fullfill organizational tasks is critical.

CULTURAL IMPACT SHEET: STAFFING Cont'd)

Variable	Potential Impact
Communication	**Low context** cultures express explicitly the criteria and methods for recruitment, selection, compensation and firing. Performance appraisals are given directly on a periodic basis with specific feedback by category of job. Criticism is direct and impersonal. **High context** cultures do not express explicitly the criteria and methods for recruitment, selection, compensation and firing. This information is embedded in the cultural context. Performance appraisals include subjective, as well as objective, components. Criticisms are communicated subtlely, to avoid embarassment, and the appraiser must know the employee well.
Space	**Private space** cultures tend to be more explicit when giving information regarding the implemention and elements of staffing. Staffing is more task-based and systematic. **Public space** cultures tend to be more implicit when giving information regarding the implemention and elements of staffing. Staffing is more relationship-based and less structured.
Power	In cultures that value **equality**, subordinates are expected to take some initiative with their bosses in terms of their training, career development and advancement. Subordinates expect their bosses to consult them and obtain their feedback. It is felt that work relationships should not be strictly prescribed in terms of appropriate/inappropriate behaviors and roles, and that authority should be decentralized. In cultures that value **hierarchy**, subordinates expect their bosses to take the initiative to train, develop and promote them. Subordinates expect their bosses to act autocratically. It is felt that work relationships should be strictly prescribed in terms of appropriate/ inappropriate behaviors and roles.
Individualism	In cultures that value **collectivism**, employees expect organizations to defend their interests in terms of retaining, developing and compensating them. People are generally not fired unless their behavior is outside moral or political bounds. Promotion is based primarily on seniority, and managers are evaluated according to how well they conform to organizational and group norms. Performance appraisal may be conducted not so much on an individual as on a team basis. Staffing policies and procedures may vary according to the individual, depending on his or her relationship to the decision makers. Compensation may be in the form of special bonuses or "perks" outside of the prescribed system. In cultures with high **individualism** values, organizations are not expected to defend and look after their employees' career interests and development. People can be fired when their skills are no longer deemed adequate. Promotion is based primarily on market value, and managers are evaluated according to how well they demonstrate leadership skills and initiative. Performance appraisal is conducted on an individual basis. Staffing policies and procedures apply universally and are systematic. Compensation is given via a prescribed system.

CULTURAL IMPACT SHEET: STAFFING (Cont'd)

Variable	Potential Impact
Competitiveness	Cultures that value **cooperation** select, train, develop, appraise and compensate employees on their ability to work well in groups, facilitate communications, demonstrate excellence in service and contribute to the overall work environment. Job satisfaction and quality of life are strong motivators. Cultures with high **competitiveness** values select, train, develop, appraise and compensate employees on their capability for independent action, leadership, task achievement, and demonstration of a strong work ethic and drive for success. Money and achievement are strong motivators.
Structure	In cultures with **low structure** values, loyalty to the employer is not seen as a criteria for promotion. Managers are selected on merit and not on seniority. There is higher tolerance for ambiguity and less need for job security. Achievement motivation is high and performance appraisal is based on task performance. In regard to training and development, there is an optimistic assumption about people's amount of initiative, ambition and leadership skills. Management careers are preferred to specialist careers; a manager need not be an expert in the field in which he/she manages. It is felt that work processes should be much less prescribed, i.e., negotiated rather than formalized. In cultures with **high structure** values, loyalty to the employer is seen as a major criterion for promotion. Managers are selected more on the basis of seniority. There is lower tolerance for ambiguity and greater need for job security. Achievement motivation is less and performance appraisal may be based on other factors besides task performance. In regard to training and development, there is a certain pessimism about initiative, ambition and leadership skills. Specialist careers are preferred to management careers; a manager must be an expert in the field in which he/she manages. It is felt that work processes should be strictly prescribed, by referring either to established procedures or to the hierarchy.
Formality	The criteria for hiring and promoting employees in **informal** cultures do not include standards for adherence to protocol (i.e., proper observation of status differences, social decorum, business rituals, etc.). **Formal** cultures tend to place more emphasis on how well an employee adheres to rules (which are generally unspoken), and acceptable self-presentation and business/social behavior.

CULTURAL IMPACT SHEET: LEADING

Variable	Potential Impact
Nature	Cultures that emphasize **control** over nature believe that individuals can change, improve, and control the organizational environment. Cultures that emphasize **harmony** with nature believe that individuals should co-exist in harmony with the organizational environment and each other. Cultures that emphasize **subjugation** by nature believe that individuals should adjust to the environment, not alter it. There is an acceptance of "place" and "fate."
Time	Managers in cultures that are characterized by a: • **Single focus** orientation to time emphasize action, schedules, following plans, obtaining and giving detailed information, and a linear approach to task achievement. • **Multi-focus** orientation to time emphasize relationships, flexibility, priority of people over schedules, more implicit information, and a holistic, non-linear approach to task achievement. Organizational leaders in cultures that are oriented to the: • **Past** tend to develop vision and mission statements that emphasize continuing the history, values and reputation that the company has achieved over the years. • **Present** tend to develop vision and mission statements that, for the most part, emphasize relatively short-term economic goals. • **Future** tend to develop vision and mission statements that focus on achieving long-term benefits.
Action	In **"Doing"** cultures, expertise and skill qualify a person to perform leadership responsibilities. In communications and negotiations, managers emphasize tasks over process. Problem solving is approached from a concrete, analytical perspective. Leaders motivate by facilitating achievement and giving recognition. In **"Being"** cultures, personal factors, in addition to expertise, qualify a leader. In communications and negotiations, managers place equal emphasis on the process and the tasks. Personal philosophy, values, style, etc., are important; without compatibilities in these areas, a manager is not viewed as an effective leader. Problem solving is often approached from a system of moral and philosophical principles. Motivation occurs more by job satisfaction and a sense of belonging.
Communication	In **low context** cultures, managers get work done through others by outlining specific goals and ways to achieve them. Communication is explicit and conflict is depersonalized. Work can proceed in the face of disagreement. Business relations do not depend so much on personal trust between individuals. Information flows along formal lines of hierarchy. Upward communications are often direct. In **high context** cultures, managers get work done through others by giving attention to relationships and group processes. Communication is implicit and conflict is avoided or dealt with indirectly. Conflicts must be resolved before work can progress. Business relations depend on trust and build slowly. Information is accessed more by informal networks. Upward communications are indirect, so as not to cause a superior to lose face.

CULTURAL IMPACT SHEET: LEADING (Cont'd)

Variable	Potential Impact
Space	In **private space** cultures, managers and employees generally do not share the same office space; space is compartmentalized. An office can be an accurate indicator of the importance of its occupant. In **public space** cultures, managers and employees share the same office space. Location or size of an office is not an accurate representation of a person's rank in the company.
Power	In cultures that value **equality**, managers exhibit participative or consultative styles. Leaders are expected to develop talent in the organization through delegating authority and responsibility. Contributing expertise is more important than authority or age in decision making. Employees are satisfied with participative superiors, feel free to offer recommendations for improvement or change, and do not like being closely supervised. In cultures that value **hierarchy**, managers exhibit autocratic or paternalistic styles. Leaders are expected to behave in ways that reinforce their authority and importance. Deference to authority and age are very important; respect for position is seen as critical to managing and controlling company operations. Employees are satisfied with highly directive superiors, are not comfortable offering suggestions for improvement, and like being closely supervised.
Individualism	In cultures that value **collectivism**, employees expect leaders to look after them. Leaders expect loyalty in exchange for protection. Management often entails management of groups. Motivation is by security, affiliation and work environment. Group or top-down decisions are the norm. In conflict situations, negotiations and problem solving sessions, individual expression is subordinate to group interests and/or authority. Conflict is seen as a negative force. In cultures with high **individualism** values, employees do not expect their leaders to look after them. Leaders expect employees to fulfill or exceed their responsibilities and defend their own interests. Management entails management of individuals. Motivation is by freedom, achievement and challenge. Individual decisions are the norm. In conflict situations, negotiations and problem solving sessions, employee initiative and expression are acceptable and expected.
Competitiveness	In cultures that value **cooperation**, the role of the leader is to facilitate mutually beneficial relationships, create a positive working environment and ensure high standards of service. There is generally lower job stress. In cultures with high **competitiveness** values, the role of the leader is to track and reward achievement as well as to model and encourage a strong work ethic. There is generally higher job stress.

CULTURAL IMPACT SHEET: LEADING (Cont'd)

Variable	Potential Impact
Structure	In cultures with **low structure** values, managers practice situational leadership styles and are more willing to take risks. Employees do not usually resist change, conflict, competition and ambiguity emotionally. The role of the leader is to provide strategy and broad guidelines; loose role and responsibility definitions are acceptable. Dissent and conflict are not necessarily seen as threatening. With employee development, managers are usually optimistic about their subordinates' initiative, ambition and leadership. In cultures with **high structure** values, managers practice consistent leadership styles and are not so willing to take risks. Employees usually resist change, conflict, competition and ambiguity emotionally. The role of the leader is to provide structure, details and clear instructions; there is a need for clear role and responsibility definitions. Dissent and conflict are often seen as threatening. In terms of employee development, managers are usually pessimistic about their subordinates' amount of initiative, ambition and leadership.
Formality	In **informal** cultures, patterns of work relations do exist but are flexible, including relations across authority levels. If organizational needs are not effectively served through formal relationships, the formalities are put aside. Leaders adopt a style that is conducive to the context. In **formal** cultures, protocol for regulating work relations is important, especially codes regarding hierarchy. Managers establish trust by adhering to business and social customs and lead from within the established framework.

CULTURAL IMPACT SHEET: CONTROLLING

Variable	Potential Impact
Nature	Cultures that emphasize **control** over nature tend to have systematic, explicit monitoring and control methods that are based on the assumption that the organizational and business environment can be engineered to meet goals. Cultures that emphasize **harmony** with nature tend to use control systems; however, the ways in which people's performance is evaluated against set standards tend to be more implicit. Harmony – as well as effective performance – is a key value. People are usually not evaluated in ways that could cause embarrassment or loss of face. Cultures that emphasize **subjugation** to nature tend to have informal control mechanisms, with routine performance checks. Little emphasis is placed on modern performance management techniques, since these methods assume the belief that one can directly control plans, schedules, and goals.
Time	Cultures that are characterized by: • **Single focus** orientation to time tend to have control systems that emphasize deadlines, detailed information, plans and linear task accomplishment. • **Multi-focus** orientation to time tend to have more flexible control systems, mostly due to the management assumption that plans and schedules should be adaptable, depending on changing priorities and circumstances. High involvement with people in the midst of tasks makes it difficult for plans to be strictly adhered to; controlling is thus less systematic. Cultures that are oriented to the: • **Past** tend to develop performance objectives and measures in keeping with customary goals, and standards. • **Present** tend to develop performance objectives and measures that are geared to the completion of short-term goals. • **Future** tend to develop performance objectives and measures in the context of long-term goals and expected benefits.
Action	**"Doing"** cultures focus not only on the tasks that need to be done, but also on the ways in which they are done. Performance management is more systematic, and a primary criterion for success is efficiency. **"Being"** cultures have a more fluid approach to task achievement. What is important is that the tasks get done; how exactly they are done is less important. Performance measurement tends to be less systematic. Criteria for success focus less on efficiency and more on effectiveness and adaptability.

CULTURAL IMPACT SHEET: CONTROLLING (Cont'd)

Variable	Potential Impact
Communication	In **low context** cultures, control is more task-driven. Performance objectives are met by following monitoring and control procedures and focusing on the tasks needed to complete the objectives. Feedback is direct, and negative evaluation is depersonalized, with a focus on rational solutions for getting performance back on track. Information regarding the various aspects of control is spelled out. In **high context** cultures, control is more process-driven. Performance objectives are met by devoting attention to the relationships and group processes that need to be in place for the objectives to be achieved. Feedback is indirect; negative evaluation is personalized. Information regarding the various aspects of control is embedded in the cultural context; few explicit rules are generally given.
Space	**Private space** cultures tend to have more formal performance checks. As managers are separated spatially from their employees, they have a greater need for more explicit performance measures. **Public space** cultures have more informal performance checks.
Power	In cultures that value **equality**, employees prefer the impersonal authority of mutually-agreed upon objectives over the personal authority of the boss. Subordinates tend to like working with their bosses to develop, implement, monitor and replan performance objectives. Employees are generally not afraid to disagree with their bosses, so two-way negotiations are effective throughout the various aspects of control. There is a management assumption that most subordinates do not dislike work. In cultures that value **hierarchy**, employees prefer the personal control of superiors over impersonal control systems. Depersonalized authority (e.g., performance objectives) does not work well; subordinates are comfortable with personalized authority (e.g., a directive or autocratic manager who will plan, monitor and control performance). Employees are generally afraid to disagree with their bosses, so two-way negotiations do not work well. There is a management assumption that most subordinates dislike work and will avoid it if possible.
Individualism	Cultures that value **collectivism** tend to exert control through shame. Group-oriented pressure (or fear of losing face and bringing shame to one's work group) discourages deviance from standards. Cultures with high **individualism** values tend to exert control by individual standards of excellence. Individually-oriented pressure (or fear of loss of self-respect) discourages deviance from standards.
Competitiveness	Cultures that value **cooperation** values may not support predominantly performance based control systems. Task performance is recognized as a standard for success; however, other standards are held as important, including team effectiveness, realization of service ideal, etc. Cultures with high **competitiveness** values support predominantly performance based control systems. Task performance as the primary standard for success is accepted.

CULTURAL IMPACT SHEET: CONTROLLING (Cont'd)

Variable	Potential Impact
Structure	Cultures with **low structure** values tend to have control systems that focus on broad – rather than explicit – guidelines. Detail is filled in through boss-subordinate negotiations. There is less resistance to ambiguity and more risk-taking. Cultures with **high structure** values support a need for more detail in performance standards, control techniques, feedback systems, etc. Elaborate formal systems that provide short-term feedback exist and serve to reduce ambiguity and risk.
Formality	**Informal** cultures view progress and improvement as more important than propriety, and therefore have few rules regarding acceptable etiquette for the controlling function. Attention is placed on meeting objective performance standards and not so much on maintaining image, status or formal relationships. **Formal** cultures place more emphasis on protocol in regard to control, particularly in regard to evaluating performance and communicating negative feedback. Generally speaking, the performance appraiser should know the appraised well; criticisms should not be phrased directly; and appropriate formalities should be observed.

SELF-AWARENESS: SKILL PROFILE

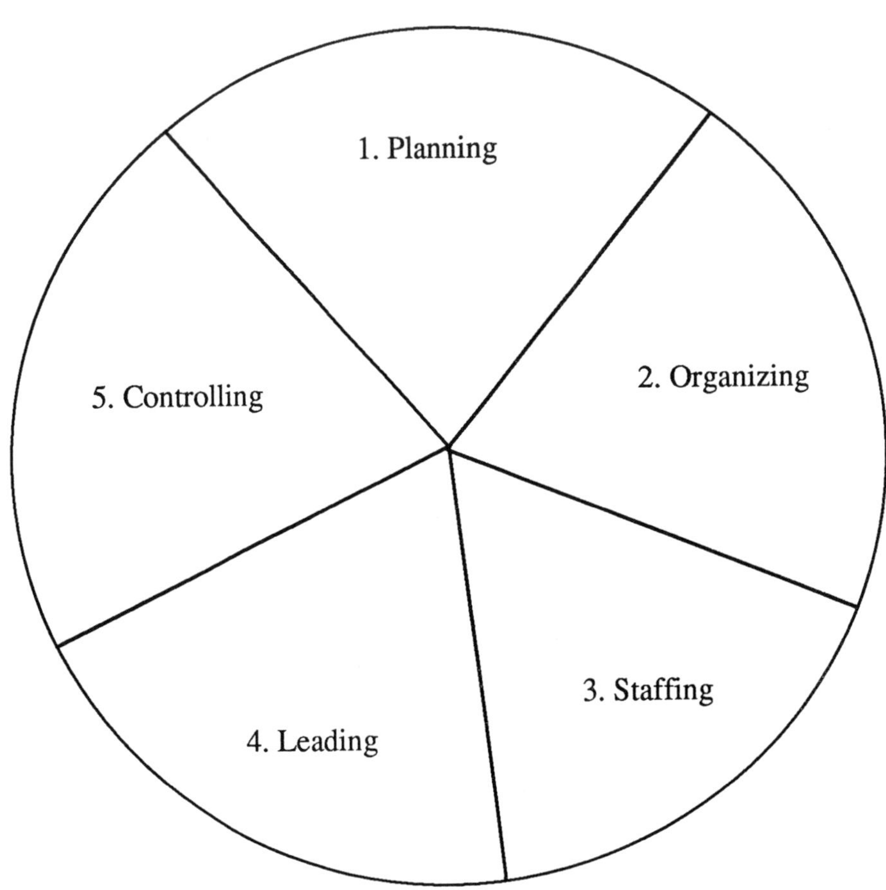

Review Question 22:

You have now reviewed the potential impact of cultural preferences on five management skills. How do you think your own cultural profile influences the way in which you perceive and perform the skills?

UNIT B: ADAPTING BUSINESS SKILLS

Objectives

After completing this unit, you will be able to:

 Determine suitable adaptations to core business skills for specific countries.

BUILDING COUNTRY PROFILES

In Module 2: Cross-Cultural Awareness, you were introduced to a three-step process for developing cross-cultural effectiveness.

- Step 1: Self-Awareness
- Step 2: Cross-Cultural Understanding
- Step 3: Adapting Business Skills

You should now have a good understanding of your own cultural orientation.

We now want you to develop culture and skill profiles for four different countries: France, Mexico, Saudi Arabia, and Germany. If you are working through the program with others, divide the task among yourselves. Use the reference materials in the Appendices to help you complete a profile. You will find suggested answers in Appendix D on pages D-14 – D-15.

Study Question 12:
What is the orientation of French culture to each of the ten variables?

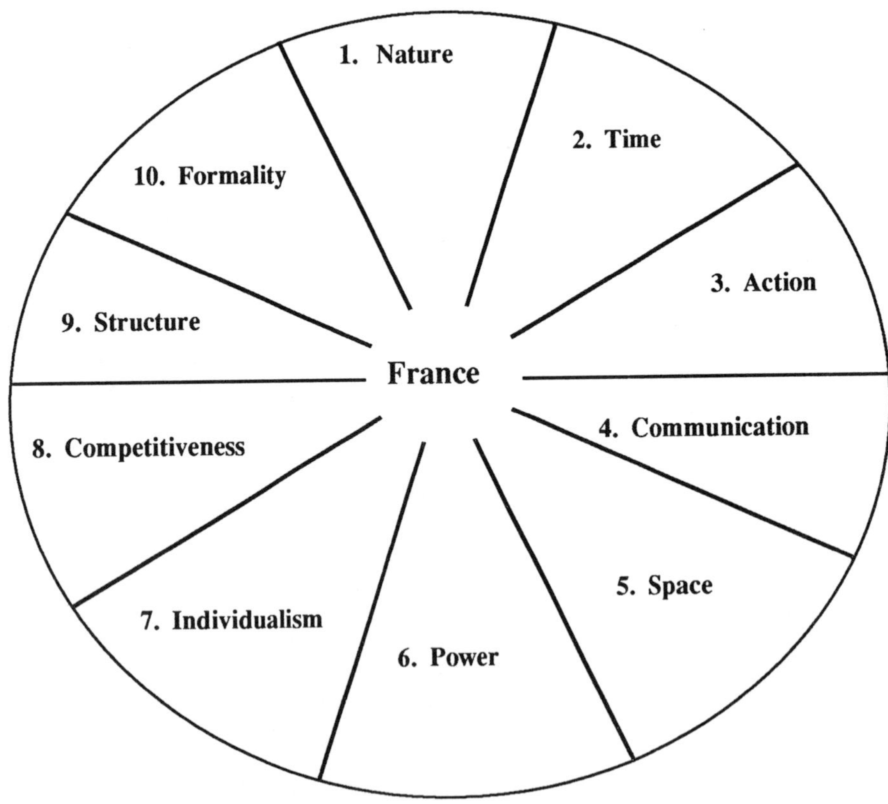

BUILDING COUNTRY PROFILES (Cont'd)

Study Questions 13-14:
What is the orientation of Mexican culture to each of the ten variables?
What is the orientation of Saudi Arabian culture to each of the ten variables?

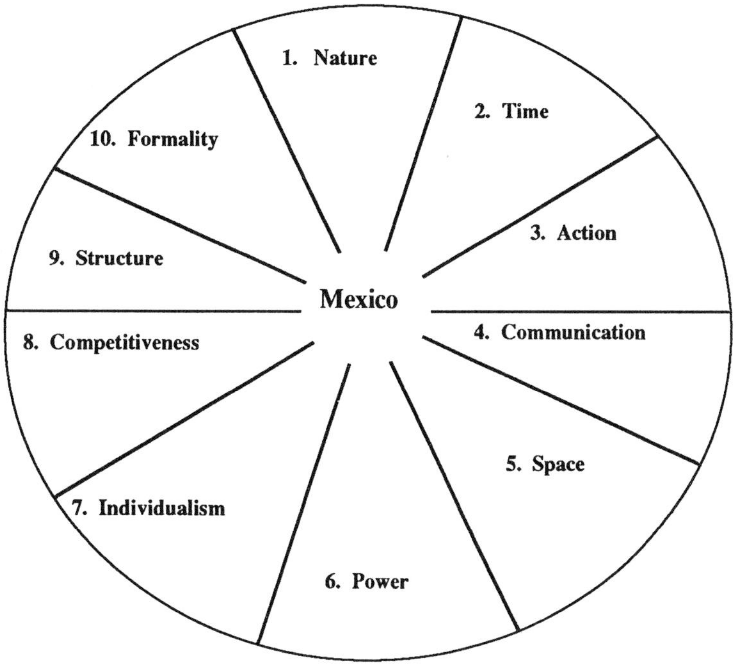

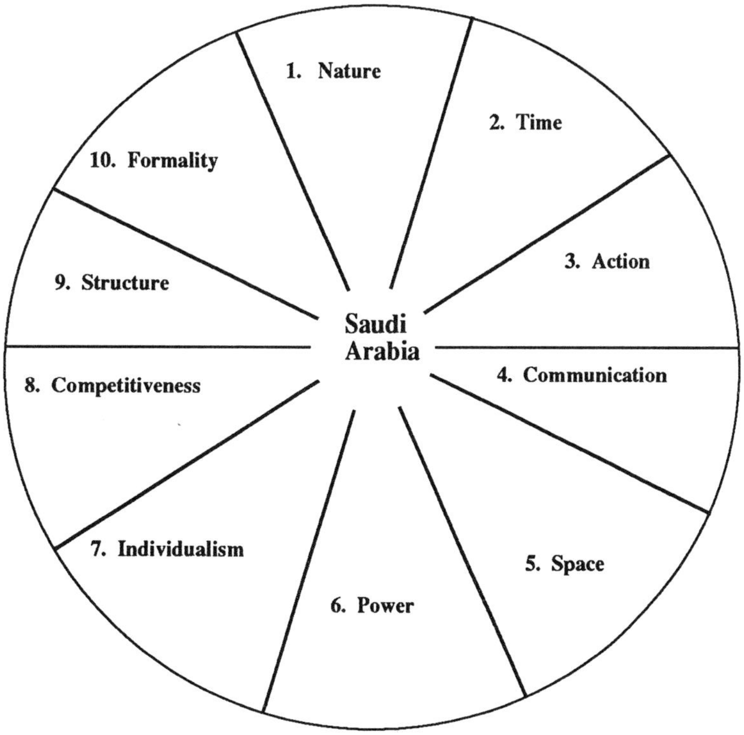

BUILDING COUNTRY PROFILES (Cont'd)

Study Question 15:
What is the orientation of German culture to each of the ten variables?

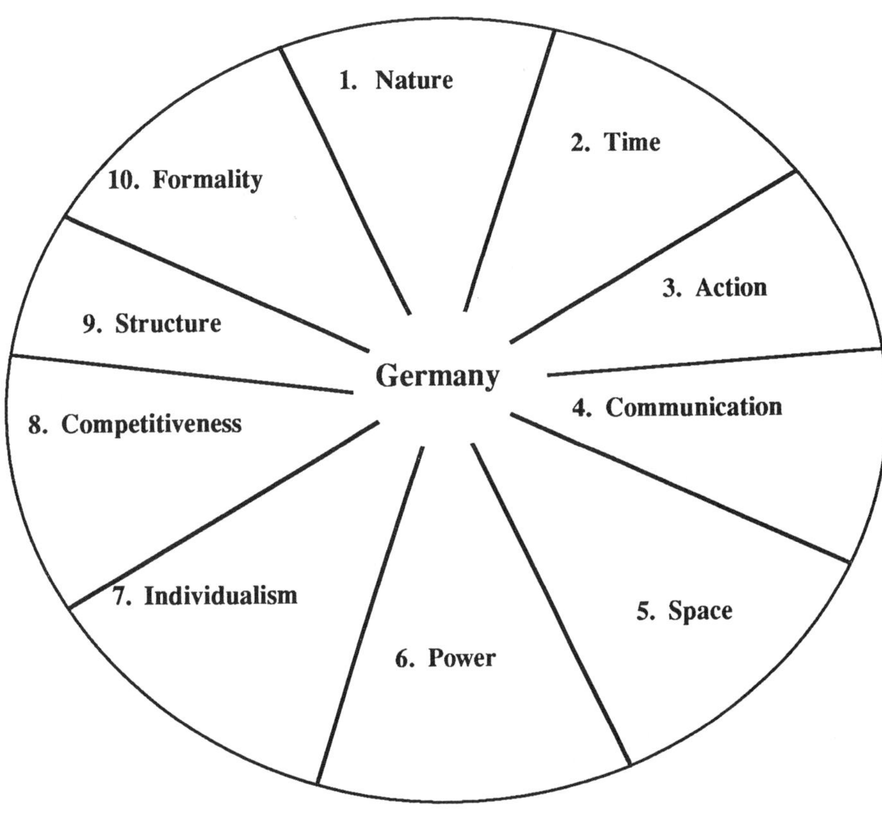

BUILDING MANAGEMENT STRATEGIES

Read through the following situation.

You are a Product Manager in your company and you want to launch a new product in a number of different countries: France, Mexico, Saudi Arabia and Germany. After talking to the subsidiaries in those countries, your Vice President of Marketing is nervous about their ability to make the launch date in nine months time.

Taking you to one side, she says, "You know how important this new product launch is to the company and I've every confidence in you to make this happen. But to be sure, I'd like you to spend at least one month in each country to put everything in place: plans, good organization, staff, appropriate controls, etc. You know what needs to be done. With the right leadership from you, they'll be able to pull this off. Just don't make waves; the last thing we need right now are angry subsidiaries."

After thinking through how you're going to tell your spouse, you ask your staff* to pull together what they know about each of the countries. Before traveling you want to identify the significant management and leadership issues you might face. You realize there are major cultural differences between your own and the other countries, and you are determined to be well prepared before you leave.

Given your own cultural profile, the cultural profile of each country, and the information on the impact of culture on several management skills, identify the key differences between your own and the foreign country in terms of: Planning, Organizing, Staffing, Leading, and Controlling. Think about how you may have to adapt your approach to each country.

Use the following page for your notes. You will find suggested answers in Appendix D on pages D-16 - D-21.

* In a group session, each team would have responsibility for a specific country. The teams – taken together – would comprise the Product Manager's staff. If you are working through this book on your own, *you* are the Product Manager's staff.

BUILDING MANAGEMENT STRATEGIES

Skill Area	France	Mexico	Saudi Arabia	Germany
Planning				
Organizing				
Staffing				
Leading				
Controlling				

UNIT C: MARKETING AND SALES

Objectives:

After completing this unit you will be able to:

- Distinguish between standardized and differentiated marketing approaches.
- Identify functions and tasks that require a greater degree of responsiveness to local needs.
- Identify the key drivers that impact the major components of international marketing.
- Avoid escalating cultural differences in sales situations.
- Recognize the need for damage control to save a sale.
- Adapt a selling style to make it appropriate to a different culture.

GLOBAL MARKETING POSITIONS

Most global business people dream of being able to sell a product across all cultures regardless of differences. For most international companies, however, the challenge is to position and present products to people in diverse markets around the world while optimizing efficiencies. Basically, there are two extreme approaches:

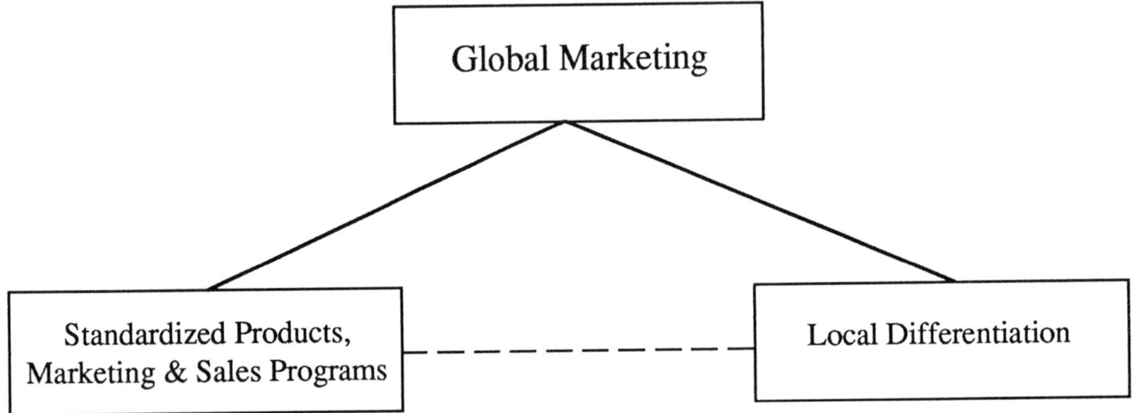

Standardized products and marketing programs provide the benefit of lower operating costs.

Many managers, however, are convinced that, because consumer and competitive conditions vary across countries, marketing strategies must be localized as much as possible.

One intermediate strategy is to regionalize, i.e., treat Latin America, Europe, etc., as marketing blocs. This integrates some of the benefits of standardization with some of the benefits of local differentiation.

There is no easy formula for deciding on an appropriate marketing and sales strategy. Each business must weigh a large number of factors, such as:

- What is our overall business strategy in terms of a centralized or decentralized structure?
- Do we achieve significant economies of scale? If so, in what areas?
- Are our products culture-bound? If so, to what extent? Products that tend to be least culture-bound are those that:
  - Are used outside the home, e.g., cars.
  - Appeal to the young, e.g., sneakers, soft drinks, jeans.
  - Are industrial, e.g., personal computers, construction machinery.
- Quality and quantity of local resources.

Most marketing and sales strategies will fall somewhere between full standardization and complete differentiation.

Review Question 23:

What is your company's current marketing strategy - standardization, differentiation or a mixture of the two? Do you see your strategy changing in the next five years and, if so, how?

INTEGRATION AND DIFFERENTIATION

In a nutshell, the challenge is to maximize brand, technology, and franchise advantages of scale around the globe, while maximizing responsiveness to the local customer. Not an easy task.

Stephen Rhinesmith, an international business consultant, provides this example of a global consumer products company.

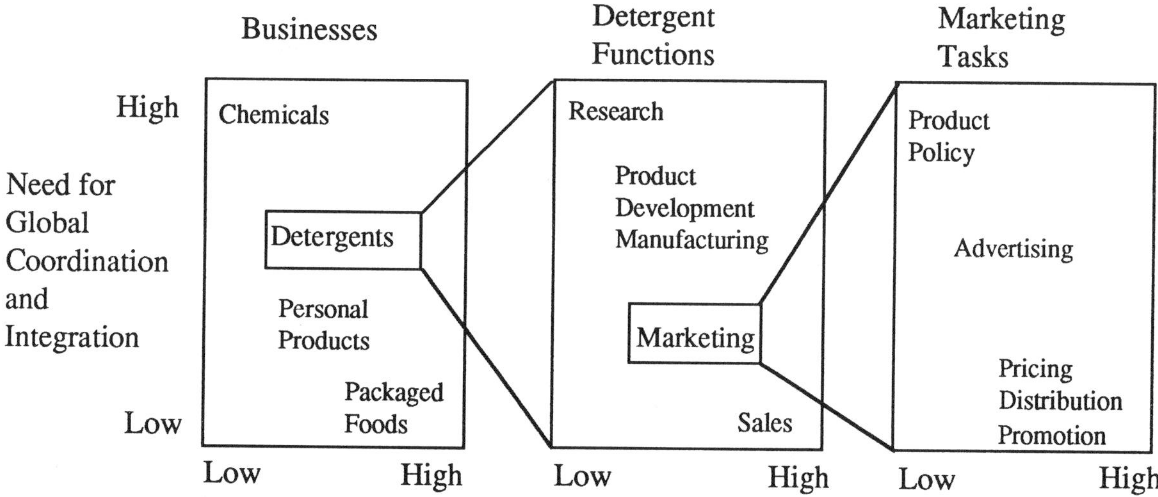

Need for National Differentiation and Responsiveness.

Source: Stephen H. Rhinesmith, *"An Agenda For Globalization."* Training and Development Journal, ASTD, February 1991.

We can see from this chart that the company considers the detergent business to have a fairly high need for global coordination and integration while requiring some need for national differentiation and responsiveness. As we follow the detergent business into its separate functions, we can see that Marketing must be responsive to the global and local needs. Sales, on the other hand, must be more responsive to local needs. As we follow the marketing function to the task level, we can see that Product Policy needs to be coordinated at the global level, while Advertising must take into account both the global and local needs. Pricing, Distribution, and Promotion must be highly responsive to local conditions.

As a rule of thumb, we can conclude: The closer an activity is to the point of sale, the more responsive it must be to local needs.

THE MARKETING MATRIX

The basic components of marketing are the same worldwide: Product, Pricing, Promotion, Distribution and Customer Service. In addition, there are certain key drivers that impact the shape of each component on the international scene: Level of Economic Development, Culture, Government, and Marketing Environment.

Here is an example of how the drivers may impact the five marketing components.

	Marketing Component				
Driver	Product	Pricing	Promotion	Distribution	Service
Economic Level	Is the consumer market fairly diverse or standardized? In general, the greater the level of industrialization, the more standardized the market.	What is the average per capita income of the target audience? • Upper class • Middle class • Lower class	What media infrastructure is available? • TV • Radio • Magazines • Newspapers	How modern is the physical infrastructure? • Railroads • Highways • Storage facilities	Is Customer Service a well developed aspect of the consumer market? What are consumer expectations?
Culture	What are the common values/behaviors? • religion • education • family structure	Is this particular product highly valued in the culture?	Who generally shops for this product? • Women • Men • Children What type of promotion is effective? • High context • Low context	What types of markets are there and where are they located? • Supermarkets vs. small operations • Many locations vs. a few centralized locations	When and how should service be delivered? • Time expectations • Private vs. public
Government	Are there restrictions on entering the market? • Trade quotas • Product specifications	Does the government put restraints on free trade? • Impose price ceilings or floors • Subsidized markets • Levy sales tax	What restrictions are there on advertising? • Government monitoring of mass media • Language restrictions	Does the government control the transportation alternatives? • Ownership of roads • Tolls	Are there regulations placed on the manufacturer? • Limited point of sales involvement
Marketing Environment	Is the product currently offered in the market? • How many companies offer the same products? • Are these products? satisfying the market?	What are competitors charging for these products? • Uniform pricing • Stability of price • Is there a less expensive substitute	What types of promotion are competitors using? How successful are they?	How difficult is it to build relationships with distributers/ suppliers?	What type of service does the competition offer?

BRINGING IT ALL BACK HOME

Think about the markets for your own products and answer the following questions:

Review Question 24:

What international markets are you currently operating in?

Review Question 25:

What plans do you have for expanding your international markets?

Review Question 26:

Which of the key drivers most impact your products?

Review Question 27:

How can your company maximize global efficiencies while satisfying local needs?

SALES: GETTING OUT OF THE ESCALATION BOX

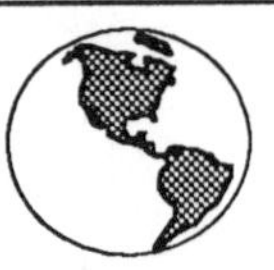

As we have seen, the sales function needs to be highly responsive to local conditions. As with negotiations, it is very easy to get stuck in a box and not be able to see a way out. How does this happen?

A salesperson and a prospect meet. Both have well established cultural orientations. The salesperson feels very annoyed when the prospect violates his or her assumptions or core values. The salesperson becomes defensive and reacts with behavior that offends the prospect. In turn, the prospect reacts with behavior that increasingly irritates the salesperson. They are stuck in the **Escalation Box** and the salesperson is likely to lose the sale.

The salesperson, as soon as he or she felt any kind of cultural friction, should have slowed down and performed a **Cultural Check** of his or her own and the other person's cultural preferences.

Meeting
Salesperson-Prospect
(culture 1) (culture 2)

Appropriate
Response

ESCALATION BOX

Cultural
Friction

Salesperson
Annoyed

Salesperson
Annoys
Prospect

Prospect
Further
Annoys
Sales-
person

CULTURAL CHECK

Examine:

Preferences
Expectations
Prejudices

Through culturally-appropriate probing questions

Increased
Cultural
Understanding

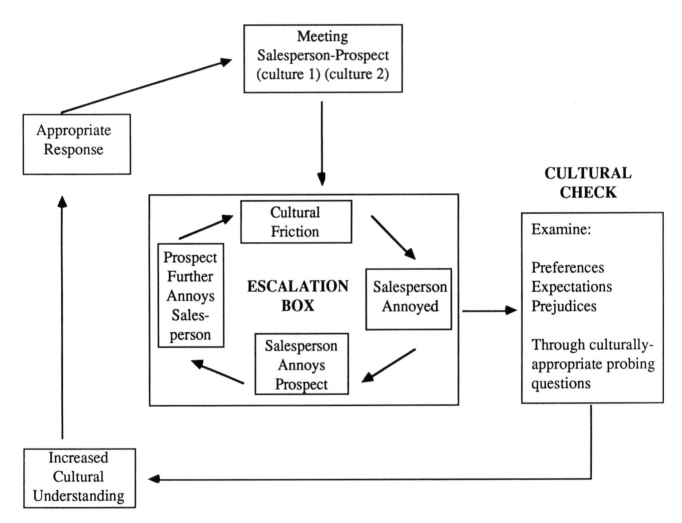

Performing a cultural check is unlikely to be a one-time event in any cross-cultural sales meeting. You may have to perform this task several times in one meeting.

DAMAGE CONTROL

Damage control is the ability to see that you have made a cultural *faux pas* and to save the situation before it's beyond repair.

It is possible that you will encounter obstacles or negative reactions in response to your attempts to modify your sales or communication style to fit the cultural background of your client. As we have already said, an individual may differ in significant ways from the dominant profile of the culture.

Examples:

1. While initiating a sales meeting with a Chinese-American, you decide to demonstrate cultural sensitivity and use a few Mandarin phrases in the conversation. Your efforts are met with a blank stare and uncomfortable silence.

   In this case, you could say something like, "Excuse me, I'm sorry – it's just that I recently learned a few words in Mandarin and have been looking for an opportunity to speak the language." Then resume your sales conversation.

2. You are talking on the telephone with a Japanese businessman and are attempting to sell him a telecommunications package. The sale is going well; from his favorable responses, you seem to have convinced him of the many merits of the plan. After he expresses satisfaction with the discount rates, you decide to go for a quick close and ask when you can install the service.

   You are met with silence, and then he makes a few vague references to "needing more time" and "needing to find out if we are ready for this." In this case, you could say, "I'm sorry if I seemed to rush you into making a decision – it's just that I know you will save a lot on your international business calls with this plan. Can I call you at a later date after you've had time to think the matter over and to consult with other members of the company?"

Confidence in responding to the customer's cues and adapting your sales approach only comes with practice. Each success you experience will increase your confidence – and you will only achieve those successes by trying. Don't hesitate to use apologies.

TWENTY-FIVE SELLING TIPS

Preparation

- Invest time in pre-sale planning: client's culture, company, industry, etc.
- Shift mindset from transaction orientation to relationship building.
- Practice presentation before the meeting.
- Know your products and services in depth.
- Arrange for uninterrupted time with the client (if possible).

Presentation

- Err on the side of formality.
- Translate features into culturally relevant benefits and communicate them early.
- Keep claims conservative and use third-party testimonials when possible.
- Don't rush, be patient, and show genuine interest in the client.
- Build trust before asking probing questions.
- Don't shout or speak quickly.
- Use standard English and avoid jargon and slang.
- Use visuals and supporting print materials.
- Don't be afraid to ask for clarification.
- Avoid the escalation box; keep revising perceptions and checking cultural assumptions.
- Defuse objections in a culturally sensitive way, and try to uncover "backstage" objections.
- Practice active listening and observing.
- Continually check to see if pace is appropriate.
- Don't cause the client to lose face.
- Don't be afraid to apologize or to explain your reasons for a different approach.
- Don't try to force a close.

Post-Sale Follow-Up

- Establish yourself as someone to serve the client after the sale is over.
- Keep building trust and rapport through adding value and relationship building.
- Work towards repeat business and referrals.
- Practice continuous improvement by reviewing successes and failures.

ADAPTING SELLING STYLES

Review the Regional Cultural Profiles in Appendix B and the critical sales incidents below. Given the appropriate regional profile, how would you adapt your selling style?

Suggested answers are given in Appendix D on pages D-22 – D-24.

Study Question 16:
How would you adapt your selling style to the cultural context?

You are a Director in New Business Ventures with an international oil and gas company. Five years ago, you were involved in negotiating an exploration deal with the Yemeni government. In the exploration program, your company located a large gas field; since then, you have been working with a Yemeni off-shore oil company to produce the gas. Currently, you are trying to locate a client for the gas. You believe you might have found a buyer – a Jordanian utility company interested in purchasing the gas and converting it into electricity.

In your dealings so far in the Middle East, you have been unsettled by the wide cultural gulf separating you from the Arabs. However, in your recent talks with the Jordanian utility company, you have been pleased to negotiate primarily with Ahmed Bedoun, a Jordanian executive who was educated in the U.S. and has had a good deal of experience doing business with Americans and Europeans. You are comfortable with his communication style and believe that you have formed the beginnings of a good business relationship with him.

You have, therefore, been a little surprised by the problems that have recently arisen in the negotiations. In your view, Ahmed and his associates have not been cooperative in discussing all the implications of purchasing the gas. This is not a simple matter of just selling the gas – it is also a matter of partnering with them to develop a four- to five-year business plan that addresses the gas, engineering and manufacturing issues involved in transportation, delivery dates, quantities to be delivered, pricing, potential involvement of Jordanian technical personnel, etc.

The Jordanian team, however, has focused soley on bargaining over price and has shown some reluctance to discussing the planning, scheduling and control issues that you really need to iron out before you can talk further about price. You have tried to speak directly to Ahmed about your business needs; but he has not seemed to understand. In fact, he has even seemed a little offended.

You aren't sure how to proceed. As much as you want the sale and believe that the relationship you have established so far is a trustworthy one, you can't go forward without a business plan.

Your answer:

ADAPTING SELLING STYLES (Cont'd)

Study Question 17:
How would you adapt your selling style to the cultural context?

You are an international sales consultant with a company that specializes in developing customized accounting software. Latin America is becoming one of your fastest growing markets, due mostly to the removal of import barriers to computers that can run sophisticated programs. You have initiated negotiations over the telephone and fax with representatives of an Argentine bank for the development of a very tailored accounting program. You are now in Buenos Aires to continue the talks in person.

Most of your communications so far have been with Carlos Alende, Senior International Manager of the Americas Region. When the first meeting began, which was 30 minutes late, Carlos immediately introduced you and your associate (Arlene Moore, technical and accounting consultant) to his boss, Eduardo Celli, and to two banking representatives. Carlos seemed to take a particular concern in making sure that everyone was properly introduced. You were a little unsettled by the delay and by the emphasis on formalities; however, the meeting went well from there. One thing that did surprise you, though, was the fact that the Argentineans were a little distant. You had expected them to be similar to other Latin Americans with whom you have done business; i.e., warmer and more personal.

At the end of the first day, Carlos asked if it would be possible for your boss to attend the remainder of the meetings; this request came from his superior. You informed him that, unfortunately, this was not possible, as your boss was in Europe and would be there for two more weeks. Besides, this project was specifically your responsibility. You also made the point that you had brought along your highly-qualified associate, Arlene, to answer any of their technical questions.

In the second round of meetings, the Argentineans continued to be as businesslike and formal as before. Things were not, however, proceeding very well. For example, Mr. Celli asked to see information that you had not been asked previously to provide and expressed frustration when you told him that you would have to send the information later after speaking with your boss.

During a break, Carlos told you that his boss was going to have to leave for a while to take care of an emergency and that he'd asked Carlos to officiate in his place. Carlos continued by saying he was sorry that the talks were not going as well as planned, but that you should not worry; the information that his boss had been asking for was just a formality (albeit a rather important one) and should not create any problems. He added that he fully supported the proposed project and that he could "say a few things to his boss to make it happen." Carlos concluded by saying he would "welcome being of help to you in other ways, especially with the Argentine banking system or the government, as you expand business further in Argentina."

You aren't sure what to make of Carlos' comments and how to proceed with the sale.

Your answer:

ADAPTING SELLING STYLES (Cont'd)

Study Question 18:
How would you adapt your selling style to the cultural context?

You are an international projects manager with a multinational health care products company. You are currently involved in negotiations to sell several chemistry analyzers, used in laboratory chemical testing, to a large German hospital. You have been working with your marketing counterpart in Germany these past few months to make the sale. He has finally obtained approval from the German hospital management to run a clinical trial for the technicians and personnel who would be using the analyzers. Based upon their clinical evaluation, management will then make the decision to purchase (or not purchase) the analyzers.

You have scheduled a trip to Munich, as part of an upcoming pan-European business trip, to meet with the German hospital team and your counterpart to plan the clinical trial and move the sale along.

At the meeting, you are surprised when the Germans present a thoroughly researched, very detailed plan of action for the clinical trial. You anticipated that the meeting would be more of a "sharing of views;" however, this is not the case. There are several key aspects of their proposal which you try to negotiate, especially in regard to the sheer number of hospital areas involved and intensive servicing required through the length of the trial. However, the Germans seem entirely inflexible. It seems that every time you try to open up points for discussion, the Germans say things like, "You are wrong," "There is only one answer to this question," or "You will do it this way." Hearing them speak this way is making you very upset and causing you seriously to question whether or not the sale is worth all the aggravation.

You are not sure how to go forward. It is highly unlikely that your management will approve the plan; as proposed, it is far more resource-intensive than a typical clinical trial. But even if the plan were approved, it might not be worth implementing, if the Germans are going to challenge you throughout the process.

Your answer:

CROSS-CULTURAL COMMUNICATION: DEVELOPMENT PRIORITIES

After reviewing the material in **Module 3: Cross-Cultural Communication**, describe what you consider to be your top three personal development priorities and those of your organization. For your personal development priorities, be as specific as you can be, e.g., description, action steps and dates.

Development Priority #1

Personal:	Organization:

Development Priority #2

Personal:	Organization:

Development Priority #3

Personal:	Organization:

UNIT D: THE INTERNATIONAL MANAGER: SUCCESS FACTORS

Objectives

After completing this unit, you will be able to:

 Identify the key Success Factors for effective international management.

INTERNATIONAL MANAGEMENT: SUCCESS FACTORS

A success factor is a skill, attitude, piece of knowledge, or personal attribute that is critical to high performance in a specific activity. We have introduced many international management success factors in this program. Here are some of the most important. You may want to add to this list.

Global Business Thinking

- Think strategically
- Develop a broad perspective on business issues
- Adopt the global manager paradigm
- Identify global business trends on a regular basis
- Analyze trends for impact and entrepreneurial opportunity

Cross-Cultural Awareness

- Know one's own culture
- Recognize and be sensitive to cultural differences
- Develop empathy
- Avoid hasty judgments
- Develop patience
- Respect differences, but don't compromise the law or core organizational values

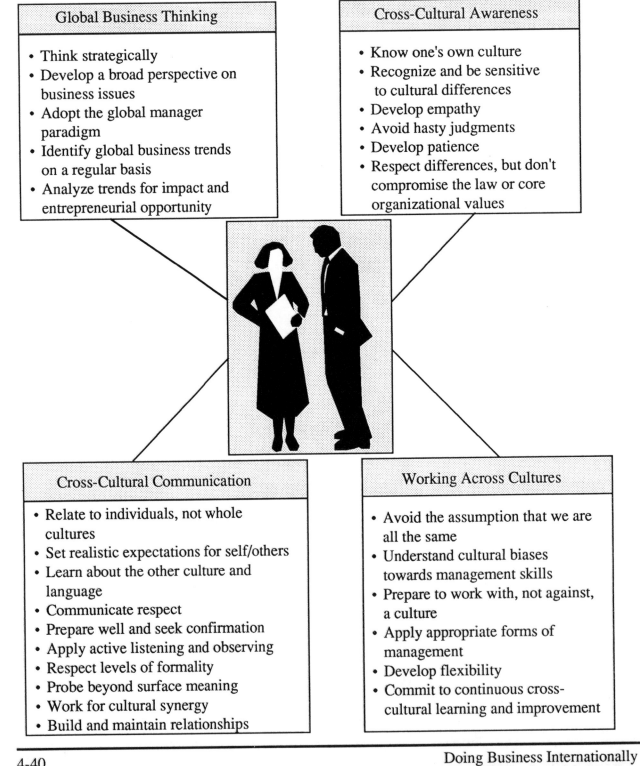

Cross-Cultural Communication

- Relate to individuals, not whole cultures
- Set realistic expectations for self/others
- Learn about the other culture and language
- Communicate respect
- Prepare well and seek confirmation
- Apply active listening and observing
- Respect levels of formality
- Probe beyond surface meaning
- Work for cultural synergy
- Build and maintain relationships

Working Across Cultures

- Avoid the assumption that we are all the same
- Understand cultural biases towards management skills
- Prepare to work with, not against, a culture
- Apply appropriate forms of management
- Develop flexibility
- Commit to continuous cross-cultural learning and improvement

APPENDICES

One of the critical abilities for the international manager is to access and use information relevant to the cultures in which he or she is doing business.

These Reference Materials provide you with information on major differences across cultures and insights into business and social etiquette within a number of countries. This information will benefit you when:

- You are planning a business trip to a foreign culture;
- You are puzzled by a foreign colleague's or employee's behavior;
- You are thinking of expanding your business overseas and you want a quick overview of some of the challenges you might face.

In the **Doing Business Internationally** program, we stress the importance of continuous learning. Keep building your reference materials and you will soon have a wealth of knowledge that will profit you in your cross-cultural endeavors. *Keep track of the trends, and the trends will soon be keeping track of you.*

NOTES

APPENDIX A: USEFUL RESOURCES

The potential list of useful cross-cultural materials is enormous. We have selected a sample that offers sound, *practical* advice for the business person.

You will learn best when you have a specific need, e.g., business trip or overseas assignment. Even on those occasions, however, you will learn more efficiently and effectively if you have maintained an on-going interest in cross-cultural business issues. Make your own additions to our list of resources; maintain a personal file of articles, reports, etc. *As the world gets smaller, your international files should be getting bigger.*

BOOKS, VIDEOS, ETC.

Books

Adler, N. J. *International Dimensions of Organizational Behavior,* Boston, MA: Kent Publishing Company, 1986.

Althen, G. *American Ways, A Guide for Foreigners in the United States,* Yarmouth, ME: Intercultural Press, 1988.

Axtell, R. *Do's and Taboos of Hosting International Visitors*, New York: John Wiley & Sons, 1989.

Bartlett, Christopher A. and Sumantra Ghoshal. *Managing Across Borders: The Transnational Solution.* Boston, MA: Harvard Business School Press, 1989.

Broganti, Nancy L. and Elizabeth Devine. *The Traveler's Guide to European Customers & Manners,* Deephaven, MN: Meadowbrook, Inc., 1984.

Central Intelligence Agency. *The World Factbook 1991*, Washington, D.C.: U.S. Government Printing Office, 1991.

Chesanow, Neil. *The World Class Executive: How to Do Business Like a Pro Around the World,* New York: Bantam Books, 1985.

Condon, J. C. *Good Neighbors, Communicating with Mexicans,* Yarmouth, ME: Intercultural Press, 1985.

Condon, J. C. *With Respect to the Japanese: A Guide for Americans,* Yarmouth, ME: Intercultural Press, 1984.

Copeland, L. and L. Griggs. *Going International*, New York, NY: Random House, 1985.

Devine, Elizabeth and Nancy L. Bragant: *The Traveler's Guide to Latin American Customs & Manners*, New York: St. Martin's Press, 1988.

Engholm, Christopher; *When Business East Meets Business East: The Guide to Practice and Protocol in the Pacific Rim*, New York: John Wiley & Sons, 1991.

Feig, John Paul *A Common Core: Thais and Americans,* Yarmouth, ME: Intercultural Press, 1989.

Foster, Dean Allen. *Bargaining Across Borders: How to Negotiate Business Successfully Anywhere in the World*, New York: McGraw-Hill, 1992.

BOOKS, VIDEOS, ETC.

Books (Cont'd)

Hall, E.T. and M.R. Hall. *Hidden Differences: Doing Business with the Japanese*, New York, NY: Doubleday, 1987.

Hall, E.T. and M.R. Hall. *Understanding Cultural Differences: Germans, French and Americans,* Yarmouth, ME: Intercultural Press, 1990.

Harris, Phillip R. and Robert T. Moran. *Managing Cultural Differences,* (Third Edition), Houston, TX: Gulf Publishing, 1991.

Hendon, Donald W. and Rebecca Angeles Hendon. *World Class Negotiating: Deal Making in the Global Marketplace.* New York: John Wiley, 1990.

Hoffman, J. *The International Assignment, Is It For You?* Foster City, CA: D.C.W. Research Associate Press, 1982.

Kohls, L. R. *Survival Kit for Overseas Living,* (Second Edition), Yarmouth, ME: Intercultural Press, 1984.

Kras, E. *Management in Two Cultures: Bridging the Gap Between U.S. and Mexican Managers,* Yarmouth, ME: Intercultural Press, 1989.

Mead, Richard. *Cross-Cultural Management Communication.* New York: John Wiley, 1990.

Mole, John. *Mind Your Manners: Culture Clash in the European Single Market*, London: The Industrial Society, 1990.

Moran, Robert T. and William G. Stripp. *Dynamics of Successful International Business Negotiations.* Houston, TX: Gulf Publishing, 1991.

Nydell, Margaret K. *Understanding Arabs: A Guide for Westerners,* Yarmouth, ME: Intercultural Press, 1987.

Rhinesmith, Stephen H. *A Manager's Guide to Globalization: Six Keys to Success in a Changing World*, Homewood, IL: Business One Irwin, 1993. (Co-published with the American Society for Training and Development, Alexandria, VA)

Ricks, D., et al. *International Business Blunders,* Washington, D.C.: Transemantics, 1974.

Stewart, E. C. and M.J. Bennett. *American Cultural Patterns: A Cross-Cultural Perspective (Revised Edition),* Yarmouth, ME: Intercultural Press, 1991.

Tyler, V. L. (Editor) *Culturgrams* (2 volumes), Provo, UT: Brigham Young University, 1984.

BOOKS, VIDEOS, ETC.

Videos

Copeland Griggs Productions: *Going International*

Part 1	"Bridging the Culture Gap"	28 minutes
Part 2	"Managing the Overseas Assignment"	29 minutes
Part 3	"Beyond Culture Shock"	28 minutes
Part 4	"Welcome Home Stranger"	14 minutes
Part 5	"Working in the U.S.A."	30 minutes
Part 6	"Living in the U.S.A."	30 minutes
Part 7	"Going International Safely"	30 minutes

Contact: Copeland Griggs Productions, 302 23rd Ave., San Francisco, CA 94121

Copeland Griggs Productions: *Valuing Diversity*

Part 1	"Manging Differences"	30 minutes
Part 2	"Diversity at Work"	30 minutes
Part 3	"Communicating Across Cultures"	30 minutes

Contact: Copeland Griggs Productions, 302 23rd Ave., San Francisco, CA 94121

BOOKS, VIDEOS, ETC. (Cont'd)

Videos (Cont'd)

Ernst & Young/MultiMedia, Inc: *The Ernst & Young Guide to the European Single Market*

Tape 1 — 21 minutes

Introduction

Part One - Europe '92

Part Two - Financial Issues

Tape 2 — 14 minutes

Part Three - Legal Issues

Part Four - External Trade

Part Five - Strategies

Contact: MultiMedia Inc., 91 Westervelt Place, Crosskill, NJ 07626

Etc.

Intercultural Press: *Current Intercultural Resources*

Listing of cross-cultural books, videos, and other materials

Contact: Intercultural Press, 16 US Route One, P.O. Box 700, Yarmouth, Maine 04096

Economist Intelligence Unit: *How-to-Guides for International Managers*

Reports on business strategies from leading international companies

Contact: Business International Corp., 215 Park Avenue South, New York, NY 10003

NOTES

APPENDIX B: REGIONAL CULTURAL PROFILES

The information on the following pages is highly summarized. It is impossible to do justice to a cultural region in a few short sentences. These profiles are just a black and white "snapshot" of richly colored cultures. You need to supplement these profiles with readings about specific countries. *Take care of the details and the details will take care of you.*

ANGLO NORTH AMERICA – U.S. AND CANADA

NATURE

The prevailing North American attitude is that human beings are superior to, and set apart from, nature. Rather than working in harmony with the natural world, Americans try to control the elements. Often they seem to be at war with nature and are less accepting of natural rhythms than people in many other cultures. This differs to some extent with Canadians, whose prevailing attitude is more a combination of mastery and harmony.

In the U.S., there is also a belief that human nature is such that men and women are perfectible and able to direct and control their personal fates. This strong self-help, individualistic, "can do" attitude is unique among the cultures of the world.

TIME

American business people value time, and there is no time like the present. Efficiency and punctuality are considered virtues, and schedules and deadlines create necessary structure. A business person's day is likely to be conducted at a swift pace, and packed with appointments. Americans have a single-focus orientation to time, and emphasize short-term productivity and goals. Canadians also tend to have a single-focus time orientation; however, as a rule, they conduct business at a less urgent pace than Americans.

ACTION

The United States is an action-oriented society – arguably the most action-oriented culture in the world. Results and actions are believed to speak louder than words, and the focus is on deadlines. Canada, as well, is more of an action-oriented than being-oriented culture; however, Canadians as a rule do not define themselves so much as Americans in terms of measurable accomplishments.

COMMUNICATION

In both countries, communication tends to be low-context, with primary emphasis on words and explicit messages.

Business communication in the U.S. is often informal, direct and explicit, and it can also incorporate a humorous tone. Business communication in Canada tends to be more formal.

In the U.S., business people are generally free to express their individual opinions, and conflict is viewed as a given – an inevitable result of individual differences and interests. Most people are comfortable with the face-to-face expression of disagreement, and conflict resolution frequently occurs by reference to law and precedent. In fact, conflict is often considered a positive force, leading to change and progress.

ANGLO NORTH AMERICA – U.S. AND CANADA (Cont'd)

SPACE

Both Canada and the U.S. tend toward private views of space and are not comfortable conducting business at too close a distance.

POWER

While Canada and the U.S. do not place a high value on hierarchy, business people from these countries do respect the authority of those in higher management levels, and maintain some distance from subordinates. While there is an acceptance of a hierarchical business structure, decisions are often based on input from different levels of the organization.

In the U.S., in particular, authority is linked to bottom-line performance. For minor decisions, majority rule is the accepted norm, and those who disagree are expected to support the decision and not be personally shamed.

INDIVIDUALISM

The United States is a highly individualistic society. The self has defined *rights* with respect to the whole. Independent individuals work together based on explicit mutual agreement, and no long-term commitment is necessarily implied. Loyalty to groups, in general, reflects individual priorities, and loyalties may change with circumstances. Nepotism is discouraged.

Canada also places a relatively high value on individualism, compared to most other cultures in the world; however, it is more group-oriented than the U.S. French Canadians are, arguably, more individualistic than Canadians from English-speaking provinces.

COMPETITIVENESS

The U.S. and Canada rate high in competitiveness. Performance counts most and advancement is rewarded on the basis of achievement. In the U.S., work tends to be extremely central in people's lives and organizational interference in one's private life is accepted. People and the environment are given more emphasis in Canada than in the U.S.

STRUCTURE

Both countries place a relatively low value on structure and do not fear uncertainty and ambiguous situations as much as in many other countries in the world. There is, however, a need for structure in business, to promote efficiency and clarity, and company rules and regulations regarding procedures are clearly specified.

FORMALITY AND INFORMALITY

American culture is comparatively very informal, in interpersonal and business circles. Canadians, particularly French Canadians, tend to be more formal than Americans.

ASIA (FOCUS ON EAST ASIA)

NATURE

Harmony with others and nature is highly valued throughout Asia.

TIME

In East Asia, attitudes toward time are single-focused, due to modernization. In Southeast Asia, however, attitudes tend to be more multi-focused.

Throughout Asia, there is both a strong past and long term future-orientation. Due to the strong connection with the past, Asians generally have a developed sense of personal identification with national and family histories. One of the implications of the emphasis on the past and family and national cohesion is that Asian cultures are more collectivistic than individualistic. Also, because Asians are generally long-term thinkers, they are particularly interested in thoroughly getting to know you and your company. Thus, negotiations can take a relatively long time.

ACTION

East Asian cultures display both “"Being” and “Doing” orientations; there is an emphasis on working very hard and achieving progress. There is also an emphasis on developing trust and relationships; business is not just a matter of accomplishing tasks. Southeast Asian cultures have more of a “Being” orientation.

COMMUNICATION

Asian cultures, in general, are high context. South Korea, however, is only moderately high. Self-expression is situational, with indirect and vague expressions common in formal situations. Direct questions, however, are often posed in both Japan and Korea. Chinese expression is more controlled. Koreans communicate somewhat spontaneously although there are slight differences between generations.

Asians tend to avoid overt conflict, valuing harmony. Symbolic confrontation is preferred to overt clashing. When disputes arise, an intermediary who knows both parties may be asked to help resolve the dispute.

SPACE

Personal space requirements are more distant than those of Latin Americans or Middle Easterners. Office spaces, however, tend to be quite public. Private offices are rare.

POWER

Asian values in regard to power tend towards hierarchy. Observance of rank is important. Differences in age, sex, and status are commonly acknowledged in deferential and honorific speech. Paternalistic authority is acceptable and acceptance of authority is a way to find personal security. In China management by committee is popular. In many Southeast Asian cultures there is usually a large “power distance” between managers and subordinates, and participatory management is not welcomed either by those with power or those on the lower levels.

ASIA (FOCUS ON EAST ASIA) (Cont'd)

INDIVIDUALISM

Individualism is not highly valued in Asia. There are, however, strong individual needs for achievement in Japan. Loyalty to the work organization is strong, as well as loyalty to parents, mentors, and past teachers.

The collectivistic orientation results in tighter teamwork, more consensual decision making and more widespread information sharing than is generally found in the U.S.

COMPETITIVENESS

Competitiveness varies across Asia. Japan, Hong Kong, and the Philippines are high in competitiveness. Other East and Southeast Asian countries rank moderate to low in competitiveness.

Achievement is highly valued in Japan and strong male dominance exists in Japan.

Even in the highly competitive Asian countries, however, there is rarely a high emphasis on individual success at the expense of the group. Achievement and performance are important, but primarily in the context of the group or team. Also, while promotion based on performance and merit is becoming increasingly important, seniority is still a weighty factor, as age and experience are highly respected.

STRUCTURE

Values regarding structure also vary. Japan, South Korea, China, Taiwan and Thailand place a relatively high value on structure. Hong Kong, Indonesia, Malaysia, the Philippines and Singapore place a lower value on structure. In general, the stronger the value of structure, the stronger the value of consensus.

FORMALITY AND INFORMALITY

Formalities are important to observe throughout Asia and extend to all aspects of doing business – greetings, business card exchange, gift giving, terms of address, negotiation protocol, dining, entertaining, etc.

EUROPE – NORTHERN AND SOUTHERN

NATURE

There is a mix of mastery over and harmony with nature, depending on the specific country. Scandinavia and the Netherlands show a particularly cooperative orientation towards the environment. Regarding attitudes towards human nature, people are seen neither as "good" or "evil" but as a mixture of the two.

TIME

There is a strong respect for tradition, and progress and change are not accorded the same importance as in the United States. More long-range goals are taken into consideration, and in this sense there is a more relaxed orientation toward time. In general, there is not the degree of short-term future urgency that one sees in the U.S.

Business people from Northern Europe have, for the most part, a single-focus orientation to time while Southern Europeans have more of a multi-focused orientation.

ACTION

Europeans value their quality of life, and this is evident throughout the culture. Family life is extremely important; leisure time is spent with the family, and month-long summer holidays are the rule.

In German and English speaking countries, work is more central; while in Scandinavia, the Netherlands and Southern Europe, work is a less central part of life.

COMMUNICATION

Communication style varies throughout Europe, being determined by the particular language and customs. Germany, Switzerland, Austria and Scandinavian countries are low context, and the rest of Western and Southern Europe is "middle context" - neither very direct/explicit nor indirect/implicit.

Most Europeans value articulate, content-driven, formal speakers. Northern Europeans tend to appreciate relatively understated presentations, while in Southern Europe and in France, eloquence is admired. Appropriate nonverbal communication, especially in regard to etiquette, helps to establish trust. There is an emphasis on face-to-face communications, especially on initial contact.

SPACE

People's respect for personal space varies with the country. Generally, people tend to be more intimate and stand closer in the Mediterranean countries, and are more reserved in the Northern European countries.

EUROPE – NORTHERN AND SOUTHERN (Cont'd)

POWER

Power orientations also vary by country. France, Belgium, Spain, Portugal and Greece place a relatively high emphasis on observing hierarchy, while the other European countries place a greater value on equality.

In general, power in organizations flows from the top down and hierarchy is recognized. Top managers usually have a high level of technical expertise. In countries that place a high value on hierarchy, authority is more centralized and executives tend to dislike power-sharing and may not communicate regularly with lower management.

The workforce is generally well trained and educated, and long tenures exist within the same company. Company loyalty and hard work are rewarded, and lateral moves between different companies can be viewed with disfavor. European managers tend to be older than their American counterparts, primarily because they do not leapfrog ranks, as Americans do.

Higher education is respected and conveys social and professional prestige. Status and class consciousness are prevalent, but less so in Scandinavia and Holland.

INDIVIDUALISM

Most European countries place a rather high value on individualism; people view themselves primarily as individuals rather than as part of a larger group. The exceptions are Spain, Portugal, Greece, Germany and Finland.

Throughout Europe, there is a distinction between one's core of intimate associates and those outside that core. This finds linguistic expression in the formal and intimate forms of address (i.e., the German use of *du* and *Sie* , French use of *vous* and *tu*, etc.). Friendships take a long time to develop and are based on emotional connections; once developed, however, they tend to be permanent.

COMPETITIVENESS

German-Swiss countries, Belgium, Greece, Italy and the U.K. place a high value on competitiveness. Spain, Portugal and France place moderate emphasis on competitiveness. The remaining Northern European countries are quite low in competitiveness and place high value on quality of life and interdependence.

STRUCTURE

Southern Europe, Belgium, France and Germany place a high value on structure and are generally risk-averse. The rest of Europe scores moderate to low in terms of structure. In the U.K. and Scandinavia, there is a higher tolerance for ambiguity (and consequently, less need for structure) than in the remainder of Northern Europe.

EUROPE – NORTHERN AND SOUTHERN (Cont'd)

STRUCTURE (Cont'd)

Decision-making in Germany entails a thorough analysis of the facts and may require more time than in the United States. The German emphasis on precision permeates much of their culture; there is an emphasis on discipline, caution and concern for detail. Group decision-making prevails in Scandinavia and the Netherlands; more centralized decision-making is the norm in Southern Europe and France.

FORMALITY AND INFORMALITY

Throughout Europe, there is an emphasis on formality and good manners. Communication and dress are customarily formal.

LATIN AMERICA

NATURE

There is a prevailing belief that human beings are controlled by forces in nature and the environment and that success is obtained not just by hard work but also by fate and luck. As economic development and secularism grow, this belief is beginning to lose its hold.

TIME

History and traditions are valued in Latin America; there is a past, as well as a present, orientation. Change may not always be viewed as positive. Also, Latin Americans tend to be multi-focused regarding time. There is overlap between business, social and family spheres; therefore, there is a flexibility regarding time and schedules, depending on shifting priorities.

ACTION

Throughout Latin America, there is a strong "Being"orientation and, therefore, a much more relaxed attitude toward action. In business, trust is established by developing long-term relationships – not just by fulfilling contracts and executing tasks.

COMMUNICATION

The communication style tends to be formal, serious, emotional and sometimes argumentative. It is high context, favoring indirect expression. Much emphasis is placed on eloquence.

SPACE

Latin Americans are comfortable doing business at closer distances than Americans, Canadians, Northern Europeans and many Asians. Latin American social distance should not be interpreted as "intimate" distance.

POWER

The majority of Latin American countries place a high value on hierarchy and rank, with the exception of Argentina and Costa Rica, which are European-influenced.

In general, predetermined roles according to age, sex and rank are strictly adhered to. Leadership style often is autocratic and authoritarian. Leaders tend to be highly experienced, well-connected senior males. Managers demand respect because of their rank, which conveys authority. There is little face-to-face questioning of authority. Conflicts are resolved by those in power. Persons in power are treated deferentially, and subordinates may not offer suggestions for improvement or be included in decision-making.

LATIN AMERICA (Cont'd)

INDIVIDUALISM

There is low value placed on individualism and high value placed on loyalty to and involvement with groups, particularly family groups. The exception is Brazil, which is quite individualistic.

In general, obligations to the family supercede all other obligations. Social relations are with family and friends, and the employer can be part of the extended family. A business may be involved with the everyday lives of its employees. Nepotism is not considered unnatural, and family considerations can, to some extent, determine employment practices. Job tenure tends to be long as firing may involve great loss of prestige.

In conducting business, rather than taking a teamwork approach, dependent workers execute tasks under the manager's direction. Competition can be seen as leading to disharmony.

COMPETITIVENESS

Competitiveness values vary widely across countries. Panama, Chile, Costa Rica, Guatemala, Peru and Uruguay are relatively low in competitiveness, i.e., emphasize concern for people and quality of life. Venezuela, Mexico, Ecuador, Argentina and Colombia are relatively high, i.e., tend more toward material success and achievement.

Even with these relatively high-competitive Latin American countries, there is still a concern for quality of life (i.e., working to live, not living to work), that is not particularly manifest in high-competitive countries in other world regions, such as the U.S. or Japan.

STRUCTURE

High value is attached to structure. Uncertainty, change and risk are generally avoided and, if faced, are dealt with by centralized or authoritative decision-making.

FORMALITY AND INFORMALITY

In Latin America, observing formality is an important part of doing business. Customs regarding hospitality, deference to authority and establishing relationships are particularly important.

THE MIDDLE EAST

NATURE

There is a prevailing belief that human beings are controlled by forces in nature and the environment. The emphasis on fate and on the will of God has vast implications for business. Because of religious fatalism, the indication that one could control the events of one's life might be viewed as arrogant or blasphemous.

TIME

The Middle East is strongly rooted in the past, its history and traditions, and in Islam. Preserving traditions and customs is emphasized over progress and change. Little emphasis is placed on developing modern management techniques.

There is a future orientation, but it tends not to be very detailed or specific, due to the belief that it is presumptuous to assume that people can control the environment. The pace of business is much slower than in the U.S., and there is less focus on efficiency.

Middle Easterners, like Latin Americans, tend to be multi-focused regarding time. There is overlap between business and family spheres, and great flexibility is demonstrated regarding time and schedules. A senior manager may be involved in many activities or different divisions simultaneously. Work flow may be interrupted by family obligations.

ACTION

There is much more of a "Being" than "Doing" orientation in the Middle East. Who a person is – and what sort of character he or she has – may be considered more important than technical merit or achievement in terms of hiring or buying.

COMMUNICATION

Communication style is high context. Speaking tone depends upon the person's social position and family influence. Face-to-face discussion or interview is the preferred mode. Negotiation and persuasion techniques are well developed. Raising the voice or displaying emotion indicates sincerity. In business communication, the source of information is as important as the content. Disputes in front of others are to be avoided.

SPACE

Middle Easterners are comfortable conducting business at a close distance – a distance that would be deemed as "personal" or "intimate" by American standards.

THE MIDDLE EAST (Cont'd)

POWER

Middle Eastern culture values hierarchical position. Status and affiliation are based on familial connections (the tribal model). Group and family determine one's role in society. Great emphasis is placed on the honor of the family name. Organizational structure is highly bureaucratic, with power and authority at the top. Leadership is authoritarian in tone, management directives are many, and instructions are rigid. A rigid chain of command exists. Leaders often deal with intermediaries or contact makers. The top manager makes all the decisions and prefers to deal only with those outside executives who have decision-making power.

INDIVIDUALISM

The Middle East places a low value on individualism. Identity is based on the attributes of the family and other in-groups more than on individual attributes. Primary obligations are to parents and family, overriding obligations to friends and work. Individual 'rights' and opinions are not emphasized.

COMPETITIVENESS

In terms of competitiveness, the Middle East lies midway, showing a balance between concern for quality of life and material success.

Succeeding in business, however, depends to a large extent on education and on being a member of a well-known and influential family. Personal contacts rather than qualifications are key for advancement, and major positions tend to be filled by those with respected social origins.

STRUCTURE

The Middle East, in general, places a high value on structure. Structure is preserved, however, more by autocratic decision-making than by establishing and following rules and regulations. Uncertain or ambiguous situations are usually considered threatening; deviant persons and ideas are considered dangerous.

FORMALITY AND INFORMALITY

As the culture is heavily steeped in tradition, certain formalities are extremely important to observe, especially in regard to the "do's and taboos" of Islam.

APPENDIX C: SELECTED COUNTRY INFORMATION

Minimize Regret: This principle should act as your guide as you seek to do business with people from another country. A single wrong gesture or remark may not cause you to lose a deal but continual rudeness and a lack of empathy might well do so. Prepare for a cross-cultural encounter with purpose and thoroughness. Take nothing for granted. *Build relationships and your business will build itself.*

Use the information in this Appendix to help you complete the International Business Quiz in Module 3: Unit B and for Building Country Profiles in Module 4: Unit B.

FRANCE

INTRODUCTIONS

Upon introduction, it is customary to shake hands with a single, quick shake and light pressure, rather than the firm American pumping handshake, which is considered boorish. It is also customary to shake hands when parting with all those to whom you were introduced.

It is best to address everyone as either "Monsieur," (Mr.) "Madame," (Mrs.) or "Mademoiselle," (Miss) without adding the surname. In business circles, first names are rarely used, even among colleagues, unless they are close friends. Use of first names can be initiated by the eldest person present, or the one with superior rank.

SOCIAL TIPS AND CONVENTIONS

Follow the same advice about conversation topics that would apply in the United States. Sports, local history and culture are generally safer topics than politics, money or personal matters.

CUSTOMARY BUSINESS PRACTICES

Business presentations should be formal, rational, and subdued.

Business negotiations in France tend to take longer than Americans are accustomed to. The French apply reason and logic to negotiations, and tend to be argumentative. At times, they may seem to disagree for the sake of discussion.

Decisions often follow a lengthy deliberation, so be patient. Trying the American hard sell could lose you a customer. An agreement may be reached orally, with written contracts to follow after approval by top management.

It is advisable to have a local agent or representative carry out the work. It may be necessary to create joint ventures, branch offices, or even a network of distributors throughout France to ensure success.

BUSINESS ENTERTAINING

Business entertaining is usually conducted in restaurants. You will probably only be invited to someone's home after you become friends as well as business associates.

Whether you are entertained at home or in a restaurant, your host would appreciate receiving a telephone call or brief note the following day, expressing your thanks.

FRANCE (Cont'd)

BUSINESS ENTERTAINING (Cont'd)

French restaurants are frequently very expensive. You should refrain from ordering the most expensive items on the menu, so as not to embarrass your host. Also, avoid the temptation to overeat – or worse – overdrink.

Spouses are seldom included at business meals. As a rule, your spouse should only be invited when you have already met your colleague's spouse.

DINING OUT

In France, cultured dinner conversation is valued as highly as the delectable food. When attending a business meal, avoid discussing business until your host indicates that it is all right to do so.

In many French restaurants, it is customary to use the same cutlery throughout the meal. If this is intended, a little glass or china rod is provided for resting the knife and fork between courses.

Smoking in public places is frowned upon. You should always ask permission before you smoke.

PUBLIC CUSTOMS

Keep in mind the French motto "toujours la politesse" (always be polite). Courtesy is valued on all levels.

GERMANY

INTRODUCTIONS

It is customary to shake hands when you are introduced or are greeting someone, and again when you are parting.

People should be addressed as Herr, Frau, or Fraulein (women under the age of 20) and the last name. First names should not be used unless that is suggested.

It is important to know and use a person's proper title. Someone with a doctorate (such as a lawyer) would be addressed "Herr Doktor X"; a professor would be "Herr Professor X."

SOCIAL TIPS AND CONVENTIONS

Germans can be formal and reserved at first meetings, and may seem unfriendly. To break the ice, you might sound out your partner for hobbies, or talk about the German countryside. Travel can also be a lively topic, since many Germans enjoy vacationing abroad.

You should be prepared to express your opinion on international events. Keep in mind, however, that politics and World War II may be sensitive subjects to Germans.

It is considered very impolite to keep your hands in your pockets while talking with someone.

CUSTOMARY BUSINESS PRACTICES

German people tend to be precise, valuing punctuality for both business appointments and private invitations. Business is conducted with great attention to detail, order and planning. Appointments should be made well in advance at the highest possible level.

Beyond normal courtesies, do not try to establish personal relationships with your business associates. Germans prefer to remain aloof until business is completed.

Business negotiations in Germany are technical and factual. It is best to avoid introducing humor, little anecdotes, surprises or a hard sell approach. Spontaneous presentations are frowned upon.

Successful business proposals and presentations are concrete and realistic, and they are best presented in an orderly and authoritative manner.

German contracts are detailed. There are two kinds of signing authority, both of which mean "by proxy." The marks "p.p." or "ppa" (per procura) indicate someone with restricted authority; "i.V." (in Vertretung) indicates a manager with full authority.

GERMANY (Cont'd)

CUSTOMARY BUSINESS PRACTICES (Cont'd)

It would be wise to participate in German trade fairs and contact the local chamber of commerce. Both are considered prestigious institutions in Germany.

Germans expect educated, responsible people to display perfect manners. This includes dressing neatly, maintaining formal decorum and practicing restraint.

BUSINESS ENTERTAINING

It is standard business practice for the customer to be invited to a business lunch or dinner. If the customer insists on hosting the dinner, this is quite acceptable. Spouses are normally only included on purely social occasions.

The evening meal is generally simple, except on special occasions and at parties.

If you are invited to a private home for an evening meal or party, the hostess would appreciate a gift of flowers. These can either be presented unwrapped before shaking hands, or delivered the following day with an appropriate message. A small bouquet of 5 or 7 flowers (uneven number), or a single blossom beautifully arranged, is usually better than a giant bunch.

The visitor is expected to make the first move to terminate the visit and should never stay too late.

DINING OUT

A German meal customarily begins with saying "Guten Appetit" to each other before eating. Drinking is preceded by the host's toasting the guests with "Prosit," or "zum Wohle." If someone raises a glass to you personally, you should reciprocate sometime during the meal.

When dining out in Germany, keep your hands on the table throughout the meal.

Men rise when a women leaves or returns to the table.

At all meals except breakfast, bread rolls should be broken with your hands rather than cut with a knife. Potatoes are eaten with a fork only, and not cut with a knife.

Smoking should be saved until the end of the meal, after the last person has finished eating, and coffee or brandy is being served. Always ask permission to smoke.

GERMANY (Cont'd)

PUBLIC CUSTOMS

Be advised that German law enforcement is strict, and fines can be imposed on the spot for such minor offenses as disregarding traffic laws. It is best not to make a fuss but to pay the fine, which is usually only a nominal sum.

Cars in Germany are extremely well cared for and often waxed and polished every weekend. When renting a car for business, keep it sparkling clean.

MEXICO

INTRODUCTIONS

When introduced to business colleagues or friends, people customarily shake hands. For closer acquaintances, a full embrace is common. It is also typical that people stand close to each other while talking.

Women often greet each other with a kiss on the cheek.

When addressing someone, use their surname unless you know the person well. Señor (Mr.) is used when speaking with a man and Señora (Mrs.) or Señorita (Miss) should precede the surname of a married or unmarried woman, respectively.

Spanish names usually include the mother's family name after, not before, the father's family name, although the father's family name is considered the surname. For instance, a man named José Rodriquez Ortega would be called Señor Rodriquez. A married woman or widow usually uses her maiden name in the middle position, as Americans often do.

SOCIAL TIPS AND CONVENTIONS

Mexicans are very proud of their country and appreciate it when visitors compliment Mexico's progress and achievements. They take these to be accomplishments on their own initiative. Avoid comparisons with the United States.

If someone sneezes, offer a "salud" (good health). The correct reply is "gracias" (thank you).

CUSTOMARY BUSINESS PRACTICES

Mexicans have a more relaxed attitude towards time than Americans do, and thus do not place a high premium on punctuality. It is not unusual for a colleague to arrive half an hour late for a business meeting.

Business is often conducted during the long midday break.

It is considered appropriate to meet with an unexpected business visitor first, even when a scheduled visitor has arrived first.

Lightweight suits are generally advisable, although winter weight suits may be worn in the evening or during winter cold spells.

MEXICO (Cont'd)

BUSINESS ENTERTAINING

Business lunches may be held between two and four in the afternoon.

In Mexico, entertaining in the home is reserved for close acquaintances. If you are invited to a private home, your hostess would appreciate receiving flowers. Take care to avoid red roses.

Even at finer hotels or restaurants, people often order mineral water. Many better restaurants serve purified iced water, because it is advisable not to drink the tap water.

For dinner a dark suit is appropriate.

DINING OUT

During the meal, both hands should be kept on the table.

Guests do not usually leave immediately after a meal.

PUBLIC CUSTOMS

As in the United States, the "thumbs up" gesture can be used to show approval.

It is considered perfectly acceptable to beckon someone with a "psst psst" sound.

As in many countries, in Mexico elderly people are treated respectfully. A gentleman on a bus is expected to give his seat to a woman or elderly person.

When paying for a purchase, place money in the cashier's hand, not on the counter.

SAUDI ARABIA

INTRODUCTIONS

In Saudi Arabia, it is customary to shake hands with everyone in an office when meeting and parting. Men often also embrace each other and kiss both cheeks. Saudi women are usually not present.

When addressing people, use the titles Mr., Sheik, Excellency (for ministers), or Your Highness (for members of the royal family) and the first name. For example, Sheik Ahmed Abdel Wahab is called Sheik Ahmed; Prince Turki Ibn Feisal is called Your Highness Prince Turki.

It is polite to accompany a visitor to the street.

SOCIAL TIPS AND CONVENTIONS

Saudi customs regarding women differ greatly from American customs. It is *not* acceptable to inquire about the women in a Saudi man's family.

It *is* acceptable to inquire about a colleague's family in general, or about his children.

Appropriate topics for conversation include admiring comments about the person's country, his city, his office, or his taste in art. However, avoid admiring an individual object, or he will feel obligated to give it to you. Politics and religion are also best avoided.

CUSTOMARY BUSINESS PRACTICES

It is not unusual to arrive for a business meeting and find another meeting already underway. It is also common practice for other people to walk in on or interrupt your meeting, and for the meeting to be reconvened several times. Although they may test your patience, the Saudis have a more relaxed attitude toward appointments. It will be necessary to tolerate frequent diversions and waiting.

A business meeting customarily begins with social conversation.

Ceremony is part of Saudi courtesy. Accept endless cups of coffee or tea.

Negotiation and bargaining is a traditional Saudi ritual. It generally begins with inflated proposals, proceeding through a series of concessions. The price should be discussed as a matter between friends, establishing trust as you proceed. Take your time, and be prepared to discuss many unresolved issues simultaneously.

To facilitate communication, eye contact and gestures of openness are important.

SAUDI ARABIA (Cont'd)

CUSTOMARY BUSINESS PRACTICES (Cont'd)

It is best to allow time for deliberation, and not press for immediate answers or a direct *yes* or *no*.

You may find it difficult to arrive at a final agreement. You should not confuse politeness with a decision. Although it is wise to get a written contract, do not be surprised if the deal is renegotiated later. Nothing is final.

Working with a Saudi agent is a good idea. Once contact is established, the agent may prefer to work directly with you and avoid middlemen. Make frequent visits to cement the business relationship.

You are better off not conducting business via the telephone or mail. It is not improper, just futile. Business is best conducted face to face.

BUSINESS ENTERTAINING

Business entertaining is usually conducted during lunch at a hotel or restaurant.

Give the local dishes a try. Your host will be delighted to explain what the different dishes are.

DINING OUT

Although Saudi meals are usually eaten with the right hand, if you are dining at a restaurant, cutlery will probably be available.

Women do not attend typical Arab gatherings.

No alcohol is served in Saudi Arabia.

PUBLIC CUSTOMS

Your passport should not read *no religion.*

Appropriate dress for men is conservative, preferably lightweight suits. People tend to cover themselves, always wearing shirts and avoiding shorts, no matter how hot the weather!

Saudi women dress very modestly, and this attitude should be respected. Women should always cover their arms and legs (wear a long skirt and a long-sleeved blouse) and dress so as not to attract attention to their bodies.

APPENDIX D: EXERCISES – SUGGESTED ANSWERS

CULTURAL VARIABLES AT WORK: PAGES 2-23 – 2-26

Study Question 1

- The key variable at work is **Action** (Being vs. Doing). That is, Italy – in comparison to the U.S. – places emphasis on "Being" and establishing and maintaining relationships in the context of business. The U.S. is, arguably, one of the most action-oriented cultures in the world, and American managers tend to focus much more on achieving measurable tasks and fulfilling contracts in business than on getting to know their counterparts, customers and suppliers personally. In many other cultures, however, business is done as much, if not more, by relationships than by the deal or contract itself.

- Another variable at work within Andrew Crowley is **Nature,** i.e., his assumptions regarding the relationship between people and the environment. Andrew, in this case, is demonstrating an unspoken belief that his one-week schedule can and should be controlled, and he experiences frustration when factors in the Italian environment throw his schedule off track.

- A final variable at work is **Time**. Italy, especially Southern Italy, tends to display a more multi-focused approach to time than the U.S. The implications of a multi-focus time orientation are the following: business is relationship-centered; plans are changed when priorities shift; and multiple things are often done while business is being done (i.e., socializing, entertaining, etc., are done while tasks are being performed, instead of being kept separate or held off until all tasks are completed).

Study Question 2

- The primary variable at work is **Communication.** The Thais, in general, tend to have much higher-context communications than Americans. That is, their communications are indirect and holistic; meaning is communicated not just by words but through a variety of contexts, such as facial expression, body language. This makes it difficult to communicate just by telephone.

- Another key variable at work is **Individualism**. According to research, Thai culture is significantly more group-oriented than the extremely individualistic U.S. culture. Therefore, there is greater need for group consensus in communications and decision-making.

- A possible variable at work is **Power.** The U.S. places less emphasis on power differences than Thailand. Therefore, the Americans in this case were possibly violating the Thais' expectations of power by asking them to participate fully in the decision-making process.

CULTURAL VARIABLES AT WORK: PAGES 2-23 – 2-26

Study Question 3

- The primary variable at work is **Structure**. According to cultural data, French managers have much higher needs for structure (due to feeling threatened by uncertain situations) than American managers. In this case, John did not show respect for Etienne Horville's needs for structure when he: a) showed that he was "making it all up as he was going along," b) did not adequately respond to his concern about the potential failure of the Training Center, and c) did not give Monsieur Horville enough time to conduct needs assessment and job analysis studies in the fashion the Frenchman deemed appropriate.

- Another variable at work is **Power**. The French, in general, feel more comfortable with power and rank differences in organizations than Americans; the combination of high structure and power needs results in a highly stratified, organizational hierarchy. John Anderson, when he asked Monsieur Horville's assistant questions that should have been addressed to Monsieur Horville alone, violated a cultural rule regarding proper channels of intraorganizational communication.

- A final variable at work is **Communication**. The "combative" style of communication Monsieur Horville used when talking to John is not necessarily indicative of ill feeling or lack of respect for John's training plans. The French educational system encourages debate between oppositional positions; conflict is not seen as undesirable but expected. Also, while both France and the U.S. are highly individualistic countries, the forms of individualism are different in both. For example, in the U.S., individualism is primarily defined in regard to inviolable rights, while in France, individualism is defined more in terms of unique differences between people. In this context, conflict can be seen as a process for upholding and respecting the individuality of others.

Study Question 4

- The primary variable at work is that of **Competitiveness.** According to research, the Netherlands is one of the least competitive cultures in the world. The Dutch, therefore, tend to stress quality of life, concern for others, supportiveness and maintaining separation between work and family/personal life. In this case, Spencer Adams, by asking Saskia Van Meer to push herself and her staff to work a significant amount of overtime on the project is, in effect, asking her to violate a strongly-felt, cultural norm.

- Another variable possibly at work is that of high-context/low-context **Communication**. The Dutch, like the Americans, tend toward low-context communications, in that explicit, direct, verbal communications are expected. In this incident, the American manager is never shown directly communicating with his Dutch counterpart on the issue of overtime but assuming that his meaning is nonetheless clear. This is a false assumption because, in this case, meaning is dependent upon a cultural norm that is not shared. Spencer Adams would have done much better to talk through work issues surrounding the campaign explicitly.

JAPANESE SCENARIO: PAGES 2-34 – 2-38

Study Question 5

Variable	Case Study Examples Illustrating Differences in the Variable
Nature	*U.S. – Control over nature; Japan, Harmony with nature.* In regard to sales, the American Director's desire to establish tighter performance controls reflects the belief that the business environment can be mastered to achieve business targets. The more implicit performance management practices exhibited by the Japanese reflect a desire to maintain harmony within the department. To enforce an explicit quota system would be to: a) focus attention more on individual performance and b) create an opportunity for lower-performing individuals to lose face. Other examples include the Japanese salespeople's perceived reticence to focus on product benefits and "go for the close" as well as the proposed introduction of an expatriate sales manager. An American salesperson would believe it is his or her responsibility to take control of the sales situation and engineer the close so that the customer is guided to make a decision. On the other hand, a Japanese salesperson might see his or her responsibility more to create rapport with the customer and provide the information needed to make the decision. In regard to bringing in an expatriate sales manager, while doing so could be the best decision in terms of ensuring control, it could be a bad decision in terms of maintaining harmony. Bringing in a *gaijin* (foreigner) could imply lack of trust in the Japanese sales manager, which would cause loss of face. A better decision would be to bring the Japanese sales manager to the U.S., which would enable him to both learn more about American sales methods and gain face.
Time	*U.S. - Present and short-term future orientation; Japan, Past and long-term future orientation.* In the "second phase of negotiations," there are differences in regard to the appropriate amount of time devoted to decision making and negotiations. The American Director is frustrated when negotiations "stretch on for months," while the Japanese require additional time to build relationships with the Director and consensus with one another. The time differences are seen clearly in the clash between the American's short-term, profit-oriented goals and the Japanese team's longer-term, partnership goals. Another example is the Director's request for a comprehensive marketing plan in less than two months. This short time frame would be not acceptable in Japan, where the development of such a plan would require much effort, involvement, research and consensus.
Action	*U.S. - Doing; Japan, Doing and Being.* The Director's plan to "continue to develop relationships with the section chiefs for the first part of his trip to Tokyo and then, during the latter part of the trip, to set forth recommendations for improvement" reflects, to some extent, that he has learned a little about Japanese/American differences. He has tried to temper his high action-orientation (emphasis on achieving organizational goals efficiently) with an awareness of the Japanese value of maintaining harmony. However, he does not temper his orientation sufficiently, as can be seen by the Japanese team's overall lack of acceptance of his recommendations. The Director did not learn beforehand about the Japanese cultural values that would clash with such action-oriented values of efficiency, change and progress, pre-eminence of task completion, etc.

JAPANESE SCENARIO: PAGES 2-34 – 2-38 (Cont.)

Variable	Case Study Examples Illustrating Differences in the Variable
Communica-tion	*U.S. - low context; Japan, high context.* Kawaguchi-san's response, "I will try," to the Director's request for a marketing plan sample is an example of high context communication. In high context cultures, information is not communicated explicitly in words but is conveyed more indirectly, through a variety of culturally understood contexts. "I will try" therefore could mean "I really cannot do that which you ask." Another example is the General Manager's message in response to all that the Director communicated in the marketing section meeting, that "Marketing is not done in Japan as it is in the West." The Director then used low context communication methods to understand exactly what the Manager meant by "pressing him to explain exactly how it was different." Not surprisingly, these methods did not work. When speaking with high context communicators, you should determine meaning by asking a series of indirect questions. The interaction between Ishihara-san and the Director in regard to the Director's recommendations for improved sales management is another good example of communication differences. Ishihara-san indirectly communicates lack of enthusiasm for these recommendations, and the Director cannot understand why he "would not at least give him the courtesy of explaining why he thought (his recommendations) were wrong." In Japan, to express disapproval directly would be very rude, as it would cause loss of face.
Space	*U.S. - private space; Japan, public space.* The American Director was surprised on two counts in regard to the sales department: that all the desks were "crowded into one office area" (and that the section chief's desk was in the same space); and that there was not a quota system to track individual output. In public space cultures, where managers and employees are in very close proximity, there is less need for formalized performance tracking; in private space cultures, where managers and employees are separate, there is more need for systematized performance management.
Power	*U.S. - equality emphasis; Japan, hierarchy emphasis.* There are two examples of the Director violating Japanese norms regarding power. The first occurred when, in the marketing meeting, he invited the Japanese team to submit to him directly their ideas about expanding OFC's business. While it is true that the Japanese frequently make suggestions to their management so as to help continuously improve the quality of the organization's internal and external functioning, such suggestions tend to flow up the hierarchy in a structured manner. Submitting recommendations first to a foreigner from outside the corporation would not be appropriate. The second incident occurred when the Director suggested that the young personnel manager reporting to Atarashi-san approach the General Manager with his recruitment ideas. Leapfrogging ranks is generally not acceptable in cultures that emphasize hierarchy. Also, in Japan, expertise is not the only factor enabling one to be recognized for ideas; age and authority level are important factors as well. A young manager might therefore feel especially uncomfortable approaching the General Manager. The manager could, however, try to have his ideas received by the General Manager either by: a) talking to him during the socializing/drinking time typically spent by Japanese workers after work hours or b) "selling" his ideas to his peers so as to form group consensus, which would carry a good deal of weight.

JAPANESE SCENARIO: PAGES 2-34 – 2-38 (Cont.)

Variable	Case Study Examples Illustrating Differences in the Variable
Individualism	*U.S. - high individualism; Japan, low individualism.* The U.S. Director in this case did not understand the impact of collectivistic cultural norms on decision-making, teamwork and performance appraisal. In the second phase of negotiations, the decision-making on the Japanese side (known as *ringi-sho*) was taking so long because of the consensual nature of the process. While Americans tend to make decisions relatively quickly and autonomously, the Japanese include all the managers (from every functional area and organizational level) involved in the implementation of the decision. In Japan, it is not uncommon for team members to compensate for their less productive co-workers. This is because the welfare of the team is seen as more important than that of the individual and group harmony is a critical value. The Director's suggestion to fire several manufacturing personnel was thus not immediately accepted. His recommendation to install a system for tracking individual sales efforts also ran counter to the Japanese collective orientation. Cultures with low individualism values tend to: appraise more on a group than individual basis; look after their employees' sense of job security; and exert control more by group-oriented (as opposed to individual-oriented) pressure. This is reflected in this Japanese approach to performance appraisal, in which people are appraised over a long period of time, in a wide range of job situations and functions, by their peers and those with whom they work closely.
Structure	*U.S. - low structure; Japan, high structure.* Members of high structure cultures, such as Japan, tend to experience stress and emotional resistance in the face of organizational uncertainty, change or ambiguity. The Director's proposal to replace the Production Department's data communications equipment so as to access information on a day-to-day basis represented a significant change to the Japanese – one that they could not immediately respond to, at least without more information explaining the full context of the proposed change. Also, the Director's discussion of his division's restructuring with the Control and Finance section chief – which provided no details of the consequences of the restructuring to the joint venture company – was another example of a low structure situation communicated in a low structure manner to a high structure receiver. As would be expected, Suzuki-san reacted in a way to offset the anxiety caused by this very uncertain news; he switched the conversation to a topic about which he could be more certain.
Formality	*U.S. - informal; Japan, formal.* In regard to observing the formalities necessary to begin a business relationship with the Japanese, the U.S. Director did fairly well. In the first phase of the negotiations, he made sure to "learn as much as (he) could about the Japanese... especially in regard to business and social etiquette... (which served him) well throughout the stages of business card exchange, gift giving, entertaining..." He also showed respect for Japanese customs when he acknowledged to the Control and Finance section chief that, while the expenses for gift giving and entertaining were more lavish than in the U.S., they were certainly necessary. But, while the Director was familiar with introductory formalities, he had not learned about the protocol involved in business communications and management. [A note on Japanese formality: while the Japanese are formal in their work relationships with foreigners, they are quite informal with strangers, family members and those with whom they work closely on a day-to-day basis. Japanese formality serves as a means to define and bridge relationships with "outsiders."]

COMMUNICATION BARRIERS AT WORK: PAGES 3-12 – 3-13

Study Question 6

- *Status*

  Mexico is a culture that places high value on power differences. Rank between organizational levels is observed and respected much more than in the egalitarian U.S. culture. Holding a staff meeting in Mexico where non-management personnel are included would be considered a breach of business etiquette – for both the support staff and management in attendance. Rank distinctions are accepted and welcomed; failing to acknowledge power differences caused Alan Richardson to lose face with all members of the department.

- *Assumptions*

  Alan made the incorrect assumption that a participative management style (i.e., inviting the department's members to give ideas for increasing sales) would be welcomed by the Mexican staff. In Mexico, due to the high cultural values regarding power, there is greater distance between the manager and the subordinate; leadership style is more autocratic than in the U.S. Rather than teamwork, workers carry out tasks under the direction of the manager in charge.

  Another wrong assumption Alan made was that the two marketing researchers, Eduardo and Miguel, would not mind being placed into competition with one another regarding looking into a marketing research system. In highly individualistic cultures, such as the U.S., tasks are given priority over relationships and group harmony; therefore, competition on the job is the norm. However, in cultures where individualism is not so high a value, such as in Mexico, motivation tends more toward affiliation than achievement, and relationships are often valued more than the tasks.

  A third assumption that the American manager made was in regard to information, i.e., that a meeting the following week to share information was appropriate. In cultures that value hierarchical differences, information is considered a managerial prerogative; information sharing is not so widely practiced, especially with subordinates present.

- *Communication Style*

  According to research, Mexicans tend toward higher-context communications than Americans. The very direct, "get to the point," efficiency-driven style of communication used by the American in the case would be considered pushy.

  Also, it was culturally inappropriate for Alan to "greet them briefly and promptly begin the meeting." In higher-context cultures, business relationships depend more on establishing personal trust. Alan should have worked on building that trust by spending a little more time in introductory conversation before plunging into the tasks at hand.

COMMUNICATION BARRIERS AT WORK: PAGES 3-12 – 3-13

Study Question 7

- *Status*

  While Great Britain does not place a high value on hierarchy per se, its aristocratic tradition and class system result in an organizational environment that observes greater distance between managers and subordinates than in the U.S. When Cynthia was leaving "messages and faxes to her co-workers expressing her need for critical input from Mr. Thomas," she was, in fact, asking them to break down a status barrier with their boss.

- *Assumptions*

  Cynthia wrongly assumed that her request would be better received if it came directly from one of the British staff members who had been working with him than from herself. In this case, she imposed her egalitarian-based assumptions on the staff members, who felt no imperative to bring their boss into the project in order to get the job done faster.

- *Communication Style*

  Here, Cynthia had not built the kind of relationship with Mr. Thomas required for her to request action and information from him. Her very low-context, task-oriented communication style was not appreciated and was thought of as "pushy." A more formal communication style, with some deference shown and protocol observed, would have been more in order, and would have facilitated Mr. Thomas's accepting her request.

INTERNATIONAL BUSINESS QUIZ: PAGE 3-16

1. When greeting a man in France, you should address him by his last name. In business circles, first names are rarely used.

2. Yes, flowers are considered to be a good gift for a hostess in Germany. However, they should be unwrapped and of a small, uneven number (5 or 7 flowers).

3. It is best to avoid discussing business over dinner in France until your host or hostess indicates that this is acceptable. Cultural conversation is valued highly.

4. It is polite to inquire about family in general or about children in Saudi Arabia. However, it is not appropriate to ask about the women in a Saudi's family.

5. In Germany, spouses are usually not included in invitations to business dinners. Spouses are normally only invited on purely social occasions.

LOST IN TAIWAN: PAGES 3-27 – 3-29

Study Question 8

Party	Values	How Values Were Manifested
Ellen	Action, Present and Short-Term Future Orientation	Found their "slow approach to business frustrating,"which, in the first trip, included time spent establishing the relationship and being entertained. Immediately followed up first trip "with extensive communications regarding developing a contract."
Taiwanese	Being, Long-Term Future Orientation, Formality	Devoted majority of Ellen's first trip to getting to know her, demonstrating a long-term commitment to a business relationship with her and her company, and observing appropriate formalities.
Ellen	Low Context Communication, Short-Term Time Orientation	Interpreted Chen Wu Ping's and his colleagues' words solely according to their literal meanings and not according to the cultural contexts. For example, she was convinced she had a firm agreement by the end of her second trip after the Taiwanese said they "looked forward to a long-lasting business relationship," praised her company's products at some length while downplaying their own, and said that "something will happen soon." Also, Ellen's short-term time orientation is apparent in her intrepretation of "soon" to mean by the end of the quarter.
Taiwanese	High Context Communication, Long-Term Time Orientation	Did not mean the above phrases to signify literally that a firm agreement would be signed. According to Taiwanese cultural contexts, these phrases would probably only signify a willingness to continue exploring the possibility of a business relationship. Also, praising others while withholding self-praise is a cultural courtesy; it did not necessarily signify that the Taiwanese believed they were getting the better part of the deal. In Taiwan, due to the longer-term time orientation, "soon" would probably not mean "by the end of the quarter."
Ellen	Control Over Nature, Low Structure, High Individualism	Believed that she could engineer the third trip so as to return with a signed contract. Was very disturbed when she could not control the timing of the Taiwanese in regard to signing the contract. Used aggressive "closing" techniques to move the contract along. She did not understand why the Taiwanese needed more time and information to make the decision and attributed their "delays" to "evading finalizing the agreement," instead of to cultural structure and group needs. Moreover, the fact that Ellen always negotiated alone represented high individualism values.
Taiwanese	Harmony with Nature, High Structure, Low Individualism	Focused on maintaining or developing harmonious relations in decision making. Thought through all the implications of the contract to ensure the contract would be in harmony with their goals and business relationships. Showed needs for guarding

LOST IN TAIWAN: PAGES 3-27 – 3-29 (Cont'd)

Party	Values	How Values Were Manifested
		against uncertainty by requesting more information, asking detailed questions and asking for more time to discuss the contract. The group orientation of the team (with no clear "acknowledged leader") also represented low individualism values.
Ellen	Low Power Values	Expected her and her company to receive respect based on their merit and expertise. It did not occur to her that her relative youth and lack of high rank in her company might hamper the deal.
Taiwanese	Higher Power Values	Chen Wu-Ping and colleagues were all much older than Ellen; this is typical of high power cultures.
Ellen	Low Context Communication	In the final meeting, she "moved quickly through the small talk," "clearly elaborated the benefits and competitive advantages of her products over the competition," "asked direct questions," and, in general, used very explicit arguments as to exactly why the Taiwanese needed to sign the contract.
Taiwanese	High Context Communication	Did not directly respond to Ellen's explicit arguments but said merely that they would "study her proposal further" and then later called in to say they would not be signing the contract.
Taiwanese	Past-Orientation to Time	Did not respond enthusiastically to the benefits Ellen outlined regarding how "her firm's products would revolutionize their somewhat-outdated methods." Change may not automatically be viewed as positive in cultures with strong historical traditions, as it is in the U.S.
Ellen	Individualism	Told the Taiwanese that, if they signed the contract, they could elicit special recognition "from their management and colleagues." This motivational appeal assumed high individualism values.
Ellen	Action Orientation	All the benefits Ellen keyed in were action-related benefits, focused on speedy progress, efficiency and keeping up with the competition. She assumed that all the Taiwanese were really interested in were the products and their action-related benefits (e.g., "Clearly, she was offering them the best products available. If they did not recognize all the advantages. . . that was their fault".).
Taiwanese	Being Orientation	The fact that the Taiwanese ended up not signing the deal, which they certainly had shown interest in, indicated that all the action-related benefits were not enough to persuade them to sign the contract. They did not sign because, ultimately, harmony and compatibility did not exist between them and Ellen. In "being" cultures, personal trust between the individuals doing business is important and helps ensure long-term business success.

LOST IN TAIWAN: PAGES 3-27 – 3-29 (Cont'd)

Study Question 9

Party	Interests/Needs
Ellen	• Making a mutually-advantageous deal; i.e., arranging for a reputable distributor to market and sell her company's products to Taiwanese companies • Getting a signed contract as quickly and efficiently as possible
Taiwanese	• Making a mutually-advantageous deal; i.e., arranging to distribute the product lines of a reputable firm to Taiwanese companies • Establishing a harmonious relationship to ensure long-term success • Maintaining the appropriate formalities • Obtaining enough information to make as informed a decision as possible • Having enough time to review the information so as to gain internal consensus.

Study Question 10

Factors that Helped

- The mutual commitment each party had to make a deal to both receive and deliver necessary products or services.

Factors that Hindered

- Irreconcilable time frames. Ellen's interest in getting a signed contract quickly was incompatible with the Taiwanese team's needs in regard to relationship-building, gathering information, making decisions, maintaining consensus, and observing appropriate formalities.

- Differences in such key cultural factors as power, action vs. being, degree of formality, harmony with vs. control of environment, individualism vs. collectivism and structure — and the lack of cross-cultural communication skills (on both sides) needed to work through these differences.

- Ellen's low-context misinterpretation of the Taiwanese high-context verbal and nonverbal communications, such as her:

  - Assumption that "Something will happen soon" meant that a contract would be signed shortly, probably before the end of the quarter.
  - Assumption that the Taiwanese team's response to her concluding remarks on the benefits and competitive advantages of her products (i.e., asking many detailed questions) signified that "the deal was slipping away."
  - Negative interpretation of the Taiwanese use of silence
  - Negative interpretation of the Taiwanese team's avoidance of eye contact when she asked them direct questions

LOST IN TAIWAN: PAGES 3-27 – 3-29 (Cont'd)

Study Question 11

She could have:

- Reframed some of the problems underlying the difficulties both she and the Taiwanese were experiencing in the negotiations.

  For example, one of Ellen's factors that hindered negotiations was the pressure she felt to get the Taiwanese to sign the contract as soon as possible. While, undoubtedly, some of this pressure was caused by her management, probably the greatest force driving her was simply "to find out conclusively whether or nor Chen Wu-Ping and his colleagues would follow through on the agreement." Ellen chose to test the Taiwanese team's commitment to future business by pressing them to close the deal; however, she could have done so through other means. Asking a series of indirect questions to Chen Wu-Ping as to what he meant when he said that "Something would happen soon," as well as spending time communicating with the Taiwanese to understand the meaning of their need for additional time and discussion of contract implications, would have helped her better understand their view of the proposed business.

- Taken more cues from the Taiwanese and adapted her business approach accordingly. This would have required her, however, to have enough cross-cultural awareness to be able to examine:

  - Why she was experiencing stress in relation to the Taiwanese; i.e., the specific behaviors or messages that were causing her confusion or anxiety.

  - Her own cultural values and expectations and how these values and expectations were being violated by the given behaviors or messages.

  - The possible values or expectations underlying the Taiwanese behaviors.

  - How she could communicate with the Taiwanese to determine correct understanding and interpretation of these behaviors.

  - What she could do to communicate respect for the Taiwanese team's key values, interests and needs more effectively.

BUILDING COUNTRY PROFILES: PAGES 4-22 – 4-24

Study Question 12

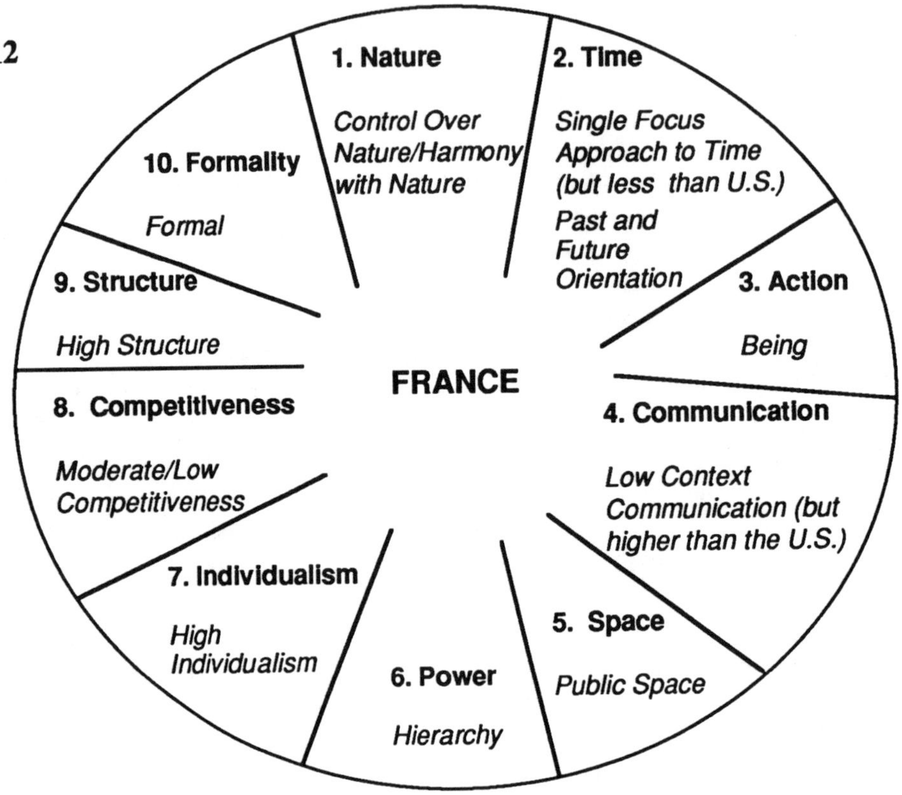

Study Question 13

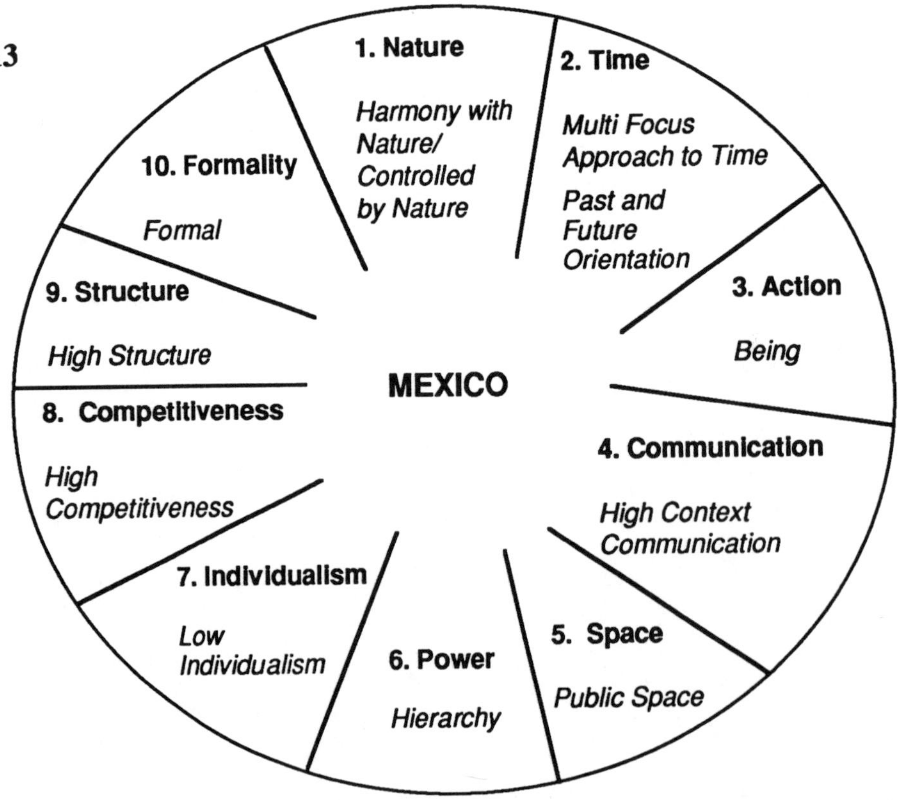

BUILDING COUNTRY PROFILES: PAGES 4-22 – 4-24 (Cont'd)

Study Question 14

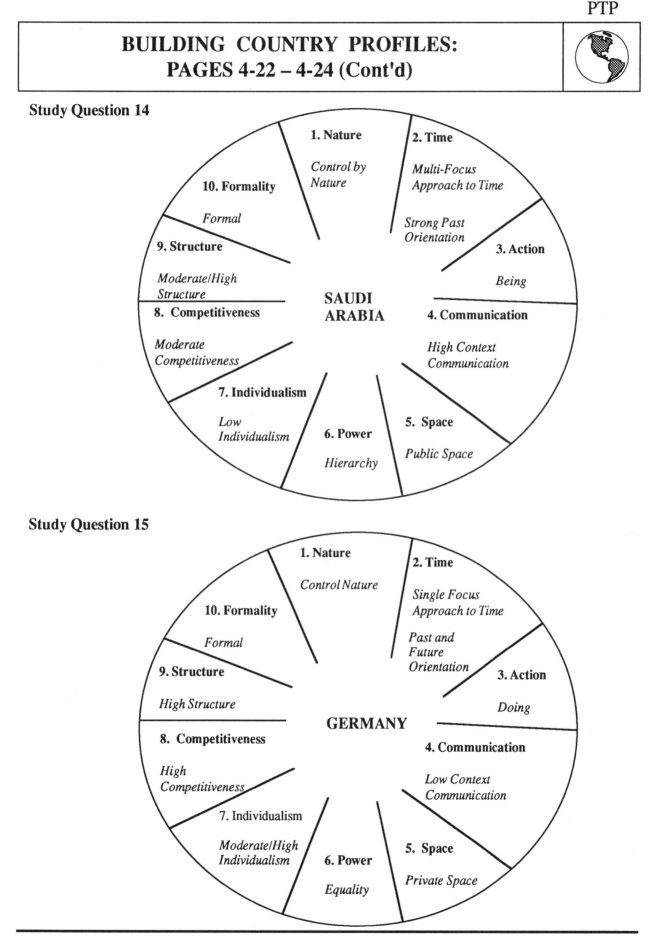

Study Question 15

BUILDING MANAGEMENT STRATEGIES: PAGES 4-25 – 4-26

FRANCE

Planning

The French past-orientation toward time (and corresponding emphasis on tradition), greater process-orientation (being), stricter adherence to hierarchy and formality, and need for structure combine to create a longer planning process than would typically exist in the U.S. As an American product manager, you should allow additional time for planning to accommodate (at least to some extent) French management assumptions. Throughout planning, you should make sure that you: a) provide structure, b) follow hierarchical channels, and c) spend time discussing the full context of the proposed plan(s).

Organizing

In the organization of work and resources, the French tend to centralize authority and responsibility, create and adhere to bureaucratic rules and procedures, and set role/task descriptions that minimize ambiguity. (This is because of the combination of high power difference and high structure needs.) You should plan to organize not just according to the criteria of maximum productivity/efficiency, but also to the cultural norms concerning respect for hierarchy, structure and formality.

Staffing

The emphasis on "being," - with high structure needs and a high value given to formality - produces an environment in which managers are not only selected and promoted based on task performance but also on other factors, such as character, self-presentation, business/social behavior, seniority, loyalty, etc. Employees expect to be developed by their superiors; there is less initiative on the part of subordinates to engineer their career development, relative to the U.S. As an American manager in France, you should (to some extent) expand your selection criteria, modify training/ development plans, and be careful about instituting quantitative performance appraisal systems. To evaluate another's performance is to make a statement about his or her personal, individual worth. Quantitative, impersonal performance appraisal could be considered very insulting to the integrity of the individual being evaluated.

Leading

An American product manager in France would be wise to: not focus solely on short-term goals; realize that the French will judge his/her leadership effectiveness not just in terms of how well he/she handles the tasks but also how well he/she manages the process; accept that managers are expected to be more directive and behave in ways that reinforce their authority; and demonstrate respect for the traditions and history of French (national, business and specific organizational) culture. Due to high structure needs, French employees tend to resist change and ambiguity. As a manager, you should take care to provide clear direction and introduce change only when you are able to provide a context for understanding and dealing with it. Also, since France is a formal culture, to build trust as a leader, you should pay attention to following social and business protocol. Finally, due to very high individualism values (and the uniquely French slant to individualism, where people express their individualism most fully through debates and the surfacing of differences of opinion), you should expect to be challenged – probably throughout the entire product launch process. Respond in kind; backing away from combative situations might cause the French to lose respect for you as an individual.

BUILDING MANAGEMENT STRATEGIES: PAGES 4-25 – 4-26 (Cont'd)

Controlling

Due to a greater "being" orientation, the French tend not to focus as much (compared to Americans) on efficiency in task completion. What is important in France is that the task be completed, not that it be completed in absolutely the most efficient way possible. Also, employees, due to a high value placed on hierarchy, prefer personal control over impersonal, management-by-objectives control. High structure needs result in a need for detail in regard to performance standards. Short-term feedback is essential for reducing ambiguity. Negative performance appraisal is never conducted impersonally and bluntly. The appraiser must demonstrate appropriate respect for the individual being evaluated, otherwise the "objective performance feedback" given will be taken as personal criticism. As an American product manager, you will undoubtedly have to adapt your management style somewhat to these expectations regarding control in order to succeed in the new product launch.

MEXICO

Planning

Due to their views toward nature, Mexicans may feel uncomfortable with a planning process that doesn't allow for flexibility concerning unforeseen events. Their multi-focus (time), being, collectivistic and public space orientations create a planning approach that focuses on developing relationships, perhaps more than the documented plan itself, to ensure plan implementation. The high context style of communication results in plans that are more implicit and less detailed. Information tends to be given on a need-to-know basis only. Due to the combination of high hierarchy and structure needs, Mexicans tend to value autocratic planning in which managers provide clear direction and instructions for plan implementation. There is an emphasis on formality; attention to rank and protocol is very important to gain support for plans.

Organizing

The multi-focus orientation to time, views toward nature and "being" produces a more unstructured, people-focused, holistic approach to organizing. Task accomplishment in the context of balancing shifting demands and environmental factors and building and maintaining relationships is the goal. Explicit documentation may be considered a waste of time, as communication is high context. Due to a combination of high hierarchy and structure values, organizational structures tend to be centralized in terms of power/authority and organizational decisions are made by referring to those in charge or to rules/regulations.

Leading

Mexicans may not share the belief that individuals can alter and control the organizational environment. Fate and luck are seen as important for achieving success. The multi-focus orientation to time, "being", and a high context mode of communication generate a business style that is relationship-focused, flexible, trust-based and more implicit. There is a non-linear approach to task achievement; people take priority over schedules. Due to high hierarchy values, leadership tends to be autocratic; workers carry out tasks under direction of the manager and are closely supervised. Subordinates generally do not participate in management or decision making. There is a strong collective orientation; obligations to the groups to which one belongs (especially to the family) may supersede work obligations and employees expect leaders to look after them. Due to high structure needs, employees tend to resist change and ambiguity and leaders are expected to provide structure and direction. In regard to formality, showing proper deference to authority is very important. Adapting your management style so as to reflect key Mexican assumptions regarding effective leadership is critical.

BUILDING MANAGEMENT STRATEGIES: PAGES 4-25 – 4-26 (Cont'd)

Staffing

Mexican views toward nature, action (i.e., "being" orientation) and time are such that purely merit and control-based staffing policies and procedures are not culturally relevant. Harmony is a key value, as well as ensuring that employees are personally trustworthy. Employment is generally long-term, firing someone is usually not an option, seniority and loyalty play an important role in promotion, family or friend considerations may factor into employment decisions, and performance appraisals are conducted more informally and personally. Due to high context communication styles, staffing criteria and methods may not be explicitly expressed. Performance appraisal tends to be more indirect as well. Due to high hierarchy and collective needs, subordinates expect that their bosses will authoritatively look after and direct their career development.

Controlling

Control is less systematic, impersonal and explicit than in the U.S., due to a combination of views toward nature, communication, action, time and space. Maintaining harmonious relations and upholding personal dignity are key values. High involvement with people in the midst of tasks may make it difficult for plans and schedules to be strictly adhered to. Control measures concentrate more on whether on not tasks are done and less so on how efficiently they are done. Attention to relationships is a primary means of ensuring that tasks are completed. Due to a combination of high hierarchy and structure values, employees are most comfortable with superiors who provide personal, directive, detailed control. Subordinates are generally not comfortable either with impersonal control systems or with participative superiors. Due to collectivistic values, exercising control through methods that result in individual recognition (positive or negative) may backfire.

SAUDI ARABIA

Planning

Due to a strong belief in the subjugation of man by nature, Saudis may view any planning process that emphasizes control over the environment as presumptuous. A combined multi-focus, being, collectivistic and public space orientation serves to create an attitude toward planning that focuses on developing relationships (as opposed to systems) to ensure plan implementation. The high context style of communication results in plans that are more implicit and less detailed. Due to the strong past orientation, traditions are upheld and change is often not embraced. High hierarchy values underlie the typically autocratic or directive style of planning; and observance of hierarchy is critical to gain support for plans. There is an emphasis on formality – attention to cultural traditions, protocol and customs is very important. You should anticipate that the Saudi team will not share some of your basic assumptions in regard to environmental control and planning. Be prepared to: a) articulate the reasons behind your approach to planning much more fully, b) deal with the "culture shock" and emotional resistance the Saudis may experience in relation to you, and c) adapt your management style to become much more people-focused. Spending time developing relationships is absolutely essential.

Organizing

Organization is not guided as much by management methods (which assume that work can be planned for) as by personal direction; this is a reflection of the belief that human beings are largely subject to forces beyond their control. The multi-focus orientation to time and "being" approach give rise to a more unstructured, people-focused, holistic

BUILDING MANAGEMENT STRATEGIES: PAGES 4-25 – 4-26 (Cont'd)

approach to organizing. Task accomplishment in the context of balancing shifting demands and environmental factors and building and maintaining relationships is the goal. Organizational communication and documentation is high context. High hierarchy values result in organizational structures that are highly bureaucratic, with power and authority centralized at the top. Due to all these cultural factors, organizing *by focusing primarily* on explicit, time-framed action steps up to the launch date could backfire – especially if, as a product manager, you do not show sensitivity to the vast American/Saudi cultural differences that impact upon organizing.

Staffing

Due to the belief that human beings are subject to environmental control, staffing decisions are not just made according to merit and task performance but also according to personal and social criteria. Ensuring the trustworthiness of an employee is essential to guaranteeing that tasks are performed in the face of inevitable difficulties. Also, as one's role in society is based on the groups and family to which one belongs, major positions tend to be filled by those with respected social origins. Firing someone may cause great loss of prestige. The implications of the "being" orientation to staffing is that people are never measured solely according to how well they perform the tasks assigned them. Staffing criteria and methods may not be spelled out and self-explanatory to someone outside the culture, as a result of high context communication values. Due to high hierarchy norms, subordinates expect that their leaders will take the initiative to train, develop and promote them; this is reinforced also by the low individualism norms of the Saudi culture. As an American product manager, you should know that firing someone should be carefully thought out and that the appropriate parties are consulted to ensure that family traditions and relationships are not violated in a way which would adversely affect your leadership position.

Leading

In Saudi Arabia, the role of the leader is not to attempt to control the environment, as is generally the case in the U.S. The strong focus on the past results in an emphasis on continuing traditions, even in the face of change. The multi-focus orientation to time, "being" approach and high context mode of communication generate a business style that is relationship-focused, flexible, implicit, process-driven, personal and trust-based. Due to high hierarchy values, leadership tends to be authoritarian; there are many management directives, employees are closely supervised and a rigid chain of command exists. Deference to authority is important. Due to the combination of strong collective and hierarchy orientations, top-down decision making is the norm and employees expect leaders to look after them in exchange for loyalty. The collective orientation can also be observed in the fact that Saudi identity is based primarily on familial connections. Thus, family obligations can override work obligations. As an American product manager, you would do well to adapt to Saudi assumptions regarding what makes an effective leader. Attention to cultural traditions and customs in the face of discharging your responsibilities throughout the product launch is imperative.

Controlling

Control is relatively informal; little emphasis is given to modern performance management techniques, as they assume one can control the environment. The multi-focus approach to time, "being" orientation, high context orientation toward communication and views toward public space create a fairly flexible, process-driven, informal approach toward control. Plans and schedules are considered adaptable to accommodate shifting priorities and needs. Efficiency is not considered a key value and attention to relationships is a primary means of ensuring that tasks are completed. Due to high hierarchy values, employees prefer the personal control of superiors over impersonal control systems. Collectivistic norms support control methods based more on group-

BUILDING MANAGEMENT STRATEGIES: PAGES 4-25 – 4-26 (Cont'd)

oriented pressure. In regard to performance appraisal, observing appropriate protocol is very important; failing to do so can cause loss of face. In managing a Saudi product launch team, it is important to adapt somewhat to their cultural expectations regarding appropriate means of monitoring and control. At the least, you should accept that the most effective way to control the project progress would be to focus on the processes and relationships involved in task completion and not the tasks themselves.

GERMANY

Planning

Due to a stronger past and future orientation, a short-term focus for planning aimed at quick results is generally not adopted or appreciated. The combination of an extremely low context style of communication and high structure needs results in a planning process that is very explicit, directive and detailed. Individualism values are lower than in the U.S.; groups or teams often make planning decisions. There is an emphasis on observing formalities throughout planning – failing to do so can result in loss of support for the plan(s). You should prepare for a somewhat longer planning process resulting in the development of a specific, structured plan.

Organizing

Past goals and precedents, as well as longer-term goals, guide the organizing process. Due to low context communication, the various outputs of the organizing process (i.e., job/task descriptions, authority relationships, monitoring/control procedures, etc.) are explicitly clear. There is high regard for structure and, consequently, organizational procedures and outputs are strictly followed. Organizational forms that allow for conflict and/or ambiguity are not desirable. Formality, especially in regard to following hierarchical channels, is very important. As a product manager, it is advisable to accommodate as much as possible to German structure needs.

Staffing

Employees are selected, developed, and trained within a longer-term time orientation. Organizational loyalty is rewarded as well as performance. Due to the low context style of communication, criticism may be communicated directly and impersonally. German firms have more of a collective orientation than U.S. firms in that employees expect their companies to look after their interests. Due to high structure needs, there is lower tolerance for ambiguity, greater need for job security, more emphasis given to seniority for promotion, and an emphasis on specialist careers. A manager must be an expert in the field he/she manages. Recognizing German and American staffing differences would be important for the product launch, especially in regard to the ways in which German employees expect to be treated by their management.

Leading

In Germany, leaders demonstrate a past and future orientation toward business goals. Communication is very explicit (low context) and conflict is depersonalized. Due to high structure values, procedures are established and strictly followed; the role of the leader is to provide and enforce structure. Formalities regarding work relations are important, especially in relation to observing hierarchical relations. As an American product manager in Germany, a more structured, formal leadership style is appropriate. Do not be surprised when those around you

BUILDING MANAGEMENT STRATEGIES: PAGES 4-25 – 4-26 (Cont'd)

explicitly inform you of the specific ways in which things are done in Germany and what you are doing wrong; this is a reflection of high structure and explicit communication cultural values – not a personal affront.

Controlling

Performance objectives and measures are not geared primarily to the completion of short term goals. Due to the extremely low context style of communication, performance feedback is direct and negative evaluation is depersonalized. Systems for monitoring and control are explicit. High structure values generate performance management systems that are formalized and detailed. As a product manager, you should expect to have your performance evaluated more explicitly than would be typical in the U.S. In managing a German product launch team, it would be important to formalize and communicate the means by which you would be monitoring and controlling their efforts; management-by-objectives is effective.

ADAPTING SELLING STYLES: PAGES 4-35 – 4-37

Study Question 12

Cultural Differences

- The primary variable at work is **Nature**. Americans generally believe that human beings should be the master of their environment while most Arab cultures believe that humans are at the mercy of their environment. The implications here for planning, organizing and control are such that:
  - The U.S. values detailed action plans to achieve business goals, particularly if the environment in which the goals are to be achieved is volatile. Project management methods are widely used to organize work and resources. To ensure that goals are accomplished, explicit monitoring and control systems are devised.
  - Most Arab cultures do value planning, but often believe it is presumptuous to develop specific, long-term plans that assume control over the environment. Organizing work and resources therefore tend to be based less on the application of modern management methods. To ensure that goals are accomplished, leaders personally conduct informal performance checks; monitoring and controlling are less systematic and explicit.
- Another variable at work is the **Doing vs. Being** dimension. The American approaches negotiations from an analytical, task-oriented perspective, while the Arab team appears to view the negotiation as an occasion to bargain over price and continue developing the relationship. "Doing" cultures negotiate more on the basis of hard information to ascertain the probability of plan implementation. "Being" cultures will often focus most on building the relationship to determine whether or not they can trust each other to carry out the proposed arrangements.
- A final variable is **Communication**. The low-context American engages in explicit communication regarding task accomplishment and planning, while the high-context Arabs are comfortable with more implicit communication and place more attention on the relationships involved.

Possible Ways to Bridge the Differences

- Focus on fostering mutual trust and demonstrating that you are committed to the long-term business relationship.
- Be aware that pressing for more explicit planning and control might be communicated as lack of trust in the relationship and lack of faith in the other side's commitment to honoring the agreed-upon goals.
- Present your needs for a more solid business plan as needs that, organizationally-speaking, must be met for the deal to be approved. Emphasize, however, that you realize that: a) you cannot plan for all things (inevitably, unplanned-for events will occur), b) you cannot totally control the outcome of plan implementation, and c) the commitment that both sides have to each other will ultimately ensure that goals are achieved.
- In price bargaining, try to connect price to items of information you require, such as schedules, quantities, etc.
- Be patient – allow yourself far more time to work out the details of the deal than you would in the U.S. It can be accomplished, but your communication should be less direct and more relationship-focused.

ADAPTING SELLING STYLES: PAGES 4-35 – 4-37 (Cont'd)

Study Question 13

Cultural Differences

- The primary variable here is **Power**. The U.S. has low power values and egalitarian business styles that de-emphasize formality, rank and position. However, Argentina has higher power values and greater respect for hierarchy and rank. Observing differences in levels of authority is critical; lack of concern for these distinctions is very rude. Here, Mr. Celli is not going to negotiate seriously with an American who is of a lower rank and status than himself. He will only make a decision after face-to-face conversations with the American's boss.

- Another variable is **Formality**. Argentine culture is very European-influenced; Argentineans identify very strongly with the European traditions regarding formalities. A typically-American, informal approach to doing business would, in general, not be appropriate.

- One final note is the issue of Carlos' offering to smooth things out with his boss and to help you do business in general in Argentina. He is probably aware of the many mistakes being made and views this as a chance to maximize the possibilities of achieving his own goals. In many cultures, the giving and receiving of favors is typical of the business relationship.

Possible Ways to Bridge the Differences

- Demonstrate greater respect for status, hierarchy and formality.

- Take Mr. Celli's request to meet with your boss more seriously. Do not be offended by the fact that, in high power cultures, competence alone often does not enable you to negotiate directly with someone your senior.

- Be better prepared in the negotiations. Do not merely prepare information specifically requested; if you are going to position yourself as an authority, you must be able to answer at least the majority of the other side's questions yourself.

- Utilize Carlos as a cross-cultural resource; he could be of help in repairing some of the damage done thus far and could perhaps educate you about how you could do business in Argentina more effectively. Realize though, in his view, that accepting his help will probably, obligate you to him. Returning his favors in the future, however, need not be an illegal or shady matter.

Study Question 14

Cultural Differences

- Four key variables are at work here in regard to the German management's style of expression: lower context **Communication**, lower **Power** values, lower **Individualism** and higher **Structure** values than the U.S. For the Germans, there is nothing disrespectful about correcting others about clearly prescribed methods; "You will do it this way" or "You are wrong" are simply factual statements.

ADAPTING SELLING STYLES: PAGES 4-35 – 3-37 (Cont'd)

The combination of high structure and low power values results in an organizational system that strictly prescribes work processes but not relationships between people; i.e., a system that works primarily through procedures that apply to everyone. Germans – who are even lower context than Americans – will communicate prescribed procedures very directly and bluntly. Furthermore, because Germans tend to be less individualistic than Americans, they often will not make statements in ways that acknowledge individual variances (e.g., "I see your point, but this is how I see it. . ."). To the American in the case, this style of communication seemed like a challenge to his/her authority as an individual; from the German perspective, it was not.

<u>Possible Ways to Bridge the Differences</u>

- Do not take the Germans' style of communicating as a personal affront; take it for what it is – a representation of business needs for directness and organization as well as a commitment to communicating the organization's methods to potential suppliers.
- Feel free to respond in kind. If you have procedures that you need to abide by but that are at variance with those set forth by the Germans, say so directly. Adopt a more serious and thorough approach to negotiating.
- Throughout the negotiations, do communicate respect for the terms and criteria of their proposed plan of action. Do not focus too much on the short-term sale, if possible. Germans, in general, tend to judge Americans as business partners for the long term.